International Conference on Big Data and its Applications (ICBDA 2016)

ITM Web of Conferences Volume 8 (2016)

Moscow, Russia
19 September 2016

Editors:

I. Balk
A. Raigorodsky
E. Nikulichev

ISBN: 978-1-5108-3281-7

Printed from e-media with permission by:

Curran Associates, Inc.
57 Morehouse Lane
Red Hook, NY 12571

Some format issues inherent in the e-media version may also appear in this print version.

Printed by Curran Associates, Inc. (2017)

For additional information, please contact EDP Sciences – Web of Conferences at the address below.

EDP Sciences – Web of Conferences
17, Avenue du Hoggar
Parc d'Activité de Courtabœuf
BP 112
F-91944 Les Ulis Cedex A
France

Phone: +33 (0) 1 69 18 75 75
Fax: +33 (0) 1 69 28 84 91

contact-edps@webofconferences.org

Additional copies of this publication are available from:

Curran Associates, Inc.
57 Morehouse Lane
Red Hook, NY 12571 USA
Phone: 845-758-0400
Fax: 845-758-2633
Email: curran@proceedings.com
Web: www.proceedings.com

TABLE OF CONTENTS

ITM Web of Conferences
Open access conference proceedings in Information Technology, Computer Science and Mathematics
A flexible, fast and efficient publication service, for an open access recording of your event and a wide dissemination of your proceedings
www.itm-conferences.org
edp open Open Access Publishing from EDP Sciences

edp sciences

ITM Web of Conferences

Statement of Peer review

In submitting conference proceedings to ITM Web of Conferences, I certify to the Publisher that I adhere to the **Policy on Publishing Integrity** of the journal in order to safeguard good scientific practice in publishing.

1. All articles have been subjected to peer review administered by the proceedings editors.
2. Reviews have been conducted by expert referees, who have been requested to provide unbiased and constructive comments aimed, whenever possible, at improving the work.
3. Proceedings editors have taken all reasonable steps to ensure the quality of the materials they publish and their decision to accept or reject a paper for publication has been based only on the merits of the work and the relevance to the journal.

Title, date and place of the conference

International Conference on Big Data and its Applications, Moscow, Russia, September 19, 2016

Proceedings editor(s):

Igor Balk
Andrey Raigorodsky
Eugeny Nikulichev

Date and editor's signature

Nov, 8, 2016

17, avenue du Hoggar - PA de Courtabœuf – BP 112 - 91944 Les Ulis Cedex A (France)
Tél. : 33 (0)1 69 18 75 75 - Fax : 33(0)1 69 07 45 17 – www.edpsciences.org

ITM Web of Conferences **8**, 01001 (2016) DOI: 10.1051/itmconf/20160801001
ICBDA 2016

New data mining technique for multidimensional aircraft trajectories analysis

Maria Solntseva-Chaley[1,*]

[1]MIPT, Moscow, Russia

Abstract. Under conditions of growing airport workload, airspace sectorization is necessary for accidents prevention. Sectorization should be performed taking into account regular traffic of aircrafts. A new data mining technique, solving the problem, is described. It allows to fulfill stable partition of aircraft intent trajectory sample into the groups (asymptotically converged beams), corresponding to the same runway approaches. Method is taking into account special geometric characteristics (curvature, torsion and multiple intersections) of multidimensional space trajectories of aircrafts.

1 Introduction

Currently, due to increasing data volume, to design methods and tools for big data rapid and automatic processing becomes a problem of great importance. New approaches are required for large data sets analysis (like unsupervised data mining or other machine learning techniques), that can recognize hidden patterns of motion and identify moving objects with similar characteristics and/or the same final targets.

In many areas, particularly, in aviation, it is necessary to process huge data sets of trajectories for monitoring, control or other purposes. Aircraft trajectory is represented by four-dimensional description of the aircraft's states with time, where state may include a position of aircraft center of mass and other characteristics of motion, like velocity, attitude and weight. So, in general, space trajectory is a multidimensional description of moving object path.

According to statistics, large number of aviation accidents takes place in extended airport area due to increased work load of air traffic management (ATM) systems. So, while air traffic is permanently increased, modernization and optimization of ATM-systems are needed to maintain high safety level.

Data mining techniques are widely used in the investigations on work load optimization in extended airport area, in particular, for air space sectorization. Sectorization is space partitioning into the sectors or zones of different controllers responsibility.

Air space sectorization should be done taking into account regular flows that are described by the samples of aircraft trajectories.

* Corresponding author: solnceva.chalei@gmail.com

DOI: 10.1051/itmconf/20160801001

Up to date, sectorization problem is solved by clustering [1] 2D-projection of aircraft 4D-trajectories, or with the help of space partitioning into the regions like Voronoi-diagrams [2].

Development of 3D-sectorization algorithm is at initial stage and associated with the problem of trajectory beams revealing in 3D-space. Trajectory beams are corresponding to the groups of 3D-trajectories with similar characteristics. For partitioning of trajectory sample into the beams such methods as PCA [3], nonparametric approach based on Dynamic Bayesian Networks [4] and spectral clustering [5] are used. The methods are based on reduction of analyzed data space dimensions.

Complexity of analyzed data space geometry which has specific curvature, torsion and multiple space intersections is demonstrated in Fig.1a. Example of two intent trajectory beams on different runways is shown in Fig.1b.

In the present work the details of a new approach to airport space sectorization which has been proposed earlier [6] are described. Current technique is based on determination of geometric asymptote tangent to multidimensional trajectory beam in the lower dimension space. Then trajectory beam is separated in the result of reverse transition to the original data space. As it will be shown further, such approach, while being applied to the analyses of radar data, allows getting stable results.

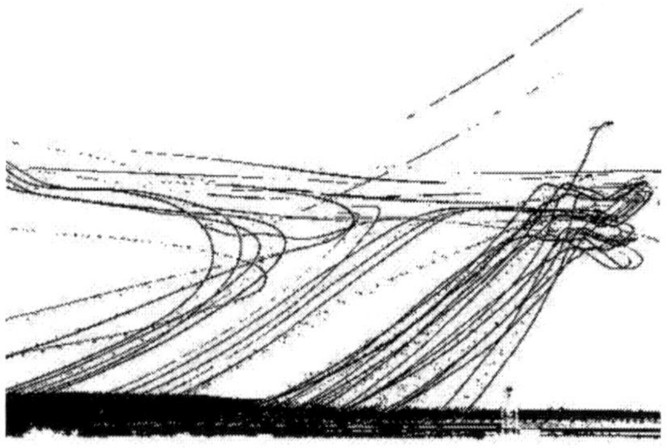

a

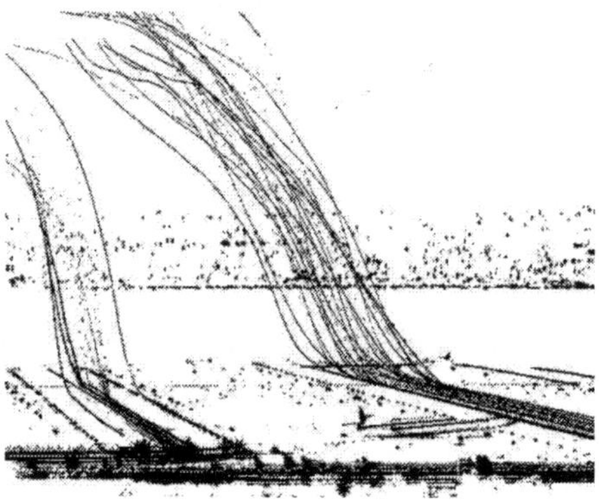

b

Fig.1 a) Intent aircraft trajectories are shown. b) Example of intent trajectory beams is presented

2 Description of analysed data

Fig. 2a illustrates analyzed sample of intent trajectories. The sample contains 116 trajectories of the aircrafts landed at the airports of San Francisco bay area 1 January of 2005 year (data is freely available at https://c3.nasa.gov/dashlink/resources/132/). Analyzed data were recorded by TRACON radar system. Reference point coincides with the radar location. Time interval between trajectory points is about 5 sec. Each trajectory consists of 160 points, as it was described in [6, 7].

 DOI: 10.1051/itmconf/20160801001

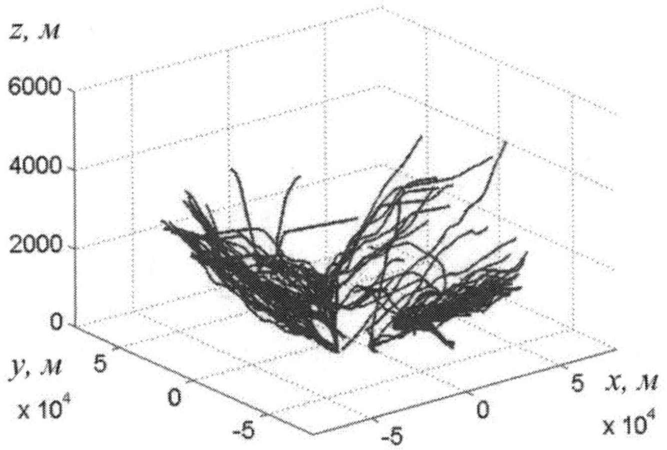

Fig.2 Analyzed sample of 4D aircraft intent trajectories is shown in 3D-space

3 Methods

3.1 Assessment of beam's asymptote

Trajectory beam $N_k, k=\overline{1,K_0}$ (K_0 is empirical parameter) is considered as asymptotically converged with a threshold parameter ε, if for all vectors $\{\mathbf{x}[i]\in R^{3\times L}, i\in N_k\}$ in the beam N_k a condition of asymptotic convergence of the beam is fulfilled

$$\forall(i,j)\in N_k,\quad \left\|\mathbf{x}[L_i;i]-\mathbf{x}[L_j;j]\right\|_2<\varepsilon, \qquad (1)$$

where $\forall i\in N_k$ $\mathbf{x}[L_i;i]$ are coordinates of final trajectory points on a runway. Parameters $L_i, i\in N_k$ are subject to determination, $\|..\|_2$ is Euclidean distance metric in three-dimensional coordinate space R^3, ε is a cutoff parameter with value of no more than runway width.

In considering the proposed approach to determination of number of converged beams, it should be taken in to account that the trajectories in asymptotically converged beams have some typical form (profile) and specific geometric asymptote in the region of convergence (1). Geometric asymptote in converged beam of multidimensional aircraft intent trajectories is a line in R^3 that meets the requirement (1). Trajectories in asymptotically converged beam have tangent line in area around their final points $\forall i\in N_k, \mathbf{x}[L_i;i]$. So, asymptotically converged trajectory beams can be identified by determination of their tangential geometric asymptotes in the points of their focuses.

Because discrete points of beam trajectories are tightly located around its' asymptote, to determine number of asymptotically converged beams sample of trajectory vectors $\{\mathbf{x}[i]\in R^{3\times L}, i=\overline{1,N}\}$ is scattered into set of the trajectories' points

$$\{\mathbf{x}[i]\in R^{3\times L}, i=\overline{1,N}\}\Rightarrow\{(x[j,i],y[j,i],z[j,i])\in R^3, j=\overline{1,L}, i=\overline{1,N}\}. \qquad (2)$$

Set of the points (2) has to be sorted according to the values of one of the coordinates (in ascending or descending order). At that, other coordinates of points, representing converged trajectory beam of certain profile, are also ordered. Then, for the scattered three-dimensional data $\{\mathbf{z}_i=(x_i,y_i,z_i),\, i=\overline{1,L\cdot N}\}$ (2) orthogonal linear regression models

$$M\ (\boldsymbol{\theta})=\{(\mathrm{x},\mathrm{y},\mathrm{z})\in\mathbb{R}^3 \mid (\mathrm{a}_1\mathrm{x}+\mathrm{b}_1\mathrm{y}+\mathrm{c}_1\mathrm{z}=\mathrm{d}_1)\wedge(\mathrm{a}_2\mathrm{x}+\mathrm{b}_2\mathrm{y}+\mathrm{c}_2\mathrm{z}=\mathrm{d}_2)\} \quad (3)$$

are analyzed by the RANSAC (*Random Sample and Consensus*) algorithm [8]. Here symbol $\wedge$ is conjunction, $\boldsymbol{\theta}=\{a_1,b_1,c_1,d_1,a_2,b_2,c_2,d_2\}$ is vector of the parameters of the models (3), that is determined under given cutoff of Euclidian distance $\rho_\perp(\mathbf{z},M\ (\boldsymbol{\theta}))$ calculated by orthogonal projection of point $\mathbf{z}=(x,y,z)$ from the set (2) onto a line $M\ (\boldsymbol{\theta})$. By such a way the model (3) is symmetrical relatively to the coordinates x,y,z. Any pair of the points from (2) is sufficiently to put forward a hypothesis about the model of orthogonal linear regression (3). Final model (3) is proved by the greatest relative quantity (percent) of scattered data $\{\mathbf{z}_i=(x_i,y_i,z_i),\, i=\overline{1,L\cdot N}\}$ (2). Algorithm MLESAC (*Maximum Likelihood Estimation Sample Consensus*) [9], that is probabilistic modification of RANSAC [8] algorithm, may be used for these purposes. The algorithm estimates likelihood of the model (3), in representing distance distribution of scattered data $\{\mathbf{z}_i=(x_i,y_i,z_i),\, i=\overline{1,L\cdot N}\}$ from the model $M\ (\boldsymbol{\theta})$ (3) as a mixture of data distributions some of which support the model (3) (inliers), while the rest ones reject it (outlier). Considering the scattered data Z (2) as independent, we obtain a relation for logarithm of likelihood as following

$$\begin{aligned} &L(\rho_\perp(\mathrm{Z},M\ (\boldsymbol{\theta}))|\boldsymbol{\theta})= \\ &=\sum_{i=1}^{L\cdot N}\log\left(\gamma p(\rho_\perp(\mathbf{z}_i,M\ (\boldsymbol{\theta}))|\mathbf{z}_i \text{ is inlier})+(1-\gamma)\,p(\rho_\perp(\mathbf{z}_i,M\ (\boldsymbol{\theta}))|\mathbf{z}_i \text{ is outlier})\right), \end{aligned} \quad (4)$$

where γ is mixing parameter. Distribution of the distances to the data, supporting the model (3), is represented by Gaussian distribution

$$p(\rho_\perp(\mathbf{z}_i,M\ (\boldsymbol{\theta}))|\mathbf{z}_i \text{ is inlier})\propto\exp\left(-\frac{(\rho_\perp(\mathbf{z}_i,M\ (\boldsymbol{\theta})))^2}{2\sigma^2}\right), \quad (5)$$

where σ is standard deviation. Distribution of distances to the data, rejecting the model (3), is described by uniform distribution

$$p(\rho_\perp(\mathbf{z}_i,M\ (\boldsymbol{\theta}))|\mathbf{z}_i \text{ is outlier})=\begin{cases}(2\rho_{\max})^{-1}, \rho_\perp(\mathbf{z}_i,M\ (\boldsymbol{\theta}))<\rho_{\max} \\ 0,\ \rho_\perp(\mathbf{z}_i,M\ (\boldsymbol{\theta}))\geq\rho_{\max}\end{cases}, \quad (6)$$

where $\rho_{\max}$ is maximal distance to data (it is defined by the context). Minimization of likelihood logarithm (4) allows to estimate vector of the parameters $\boldsymbol{\theta}$ and mixing parameter γ (see Eq. (21) in [9]). Estimation of the parameters is traditionally done using EM-algorithm [10]. Example of the algorithm practical realization in Matlab can be found in [11].

The most likely linear regression of the scattered data of trajectory sample defines geometric asymptote $M\ (\boldsymbol{\theta})[k],\, k=\overline{1,K}$ (3) of one of the sample beams under condition (1). Geometric asymptote obtained in such a manner meets the requirement

$$\forall k=\overline{1,K},\, \forall i\in \mathrm{N}_k,\ \|M\ (\boldsymbol{\theta})[L_k,k]-\mathbf{x}[L_i;i]\|_2<\varepsilon\,.$$

3.2 Separation of trajectory beam

Beams of the trajectories tangential to the corresponding geometric asymptotes are defined in the result of minimization of a cost function

$$J = \underset{\{M(\boldsymbol{\theta})[k], k=\overline{1,K}\}}{\arg\min} \sum_{i=1}^{N}\sum_{k=1}^{K} r[i;k]\rho^2_{\text{cosin}}\left(\mathbf{x}[i], M(\boldsymbol{\theta})[k]\right),$$

where $\{r[i;k] \in \{0,1\}, k = \overline{1,K}\}, i = \overline{1,N}$ is a set of binary indicator variables (e.g., if vector $\mathbf{x}[i]$ was attributed to the beam k, then $r[i;k] = 1$ and $r[i;k] = 0$, otherwise). Distance between each geometric asymptote and sample's trajectories is calculated according to cosine measure

$$\rho_{\text{cosin}}\left(\mathbf{x}, M(\boldsymbol{\theta})[k]\right) = \left(\mathbf{x}\cdot M(\boldsymbol{\theta})[k]\right) \Big/ \left(\sqrt{(\mathbf{x}\cdot\mathbf{x})}\sqrt{\left(M(\boldsymbol{\theta})[k]\cdot M(\boldsymbol{\theta})[k]\right)}\right).$$

After elimination of the points, representing the trajectories of separated beam, from the scattered data (2), the procedure of geometrical asymptote detection is repeated and the next trajectory beam is separated. In this case, remained scattered data (2) are sorted with respect to another space coordinate (different from previous one), as the model determination should be symmetric relatively to the coordinates x, y, z. The possible dependence of result (3) from coordinate directions is obviated by changing direction of data ordering in (2) from ascending to descending order or vice versa. Analysis of trajectory sample is completed, when all beams in the sample are separated.

In general, the approach described in the present work consists of two stages. Sufficient reduction of data dimensions at the first stage simplifies the revealing of data specific features. In considering 2D-projection of scattered points of 3D trajectories, the most likelihood orthogonal linear regression of the scattered data which corresponds to geometrical asymptote of one of the beams in analyzed sample of the trajectories is defined. At the second stage of the approach, after reverse transferring into the original dimensional space, a certain beam is separated from the analyzed trajectory sample in accordance with proximity (by cosine measure) to defined asymptote. Thus, due to such approach no information about the original data is lost.

4 Demonstration of the results

Earlier [7], sample of multidimensional aircraft intent trajectories was divided into subsamples in 3D-space with the help of method of polynomial regressions [12]. However, the subsamples obtained in the result are not homogeneous, as each subsample consists of several trajectory beams. Besides, the number of beams in the method of polynomial regressions is needed to be specified preliminary and the result obtained is not stable. Method described in the present work is unsupervised, so no knowledge about number of trajectory beams in original sample is necessary. In addition, this method gives stable results.

Fig.3 illustrates the stages of described technique allowing to divide one of the subsample, earlier obtained in [7], into asymptotically converged beams (see Fig.3d). Fig.3a shows two-dimensional projection of scattered data (aligned with time) of analyzed trajectory subsample. Fig.3b illustrates the result of data's linear regression using RANSAC [8] algorithm. The defined asymptote (long blue line) of the first beam is represented in Fig.3c. The beam highlighted in blue in Fig.3d corresponds to the asymptote of the same colour in Fig.3c. It should be noted that in this case the results of

 DOI: 10.1051/itmconf/20160801001

orthogonal linear regression of scattered and full trajectory data coincide. Trajectories of the first beam (see Fig.3d) are separated from the subsample mentioned above according to proximity of the trajectories to the asymptote (see Fig3c) in according with cosine measure.

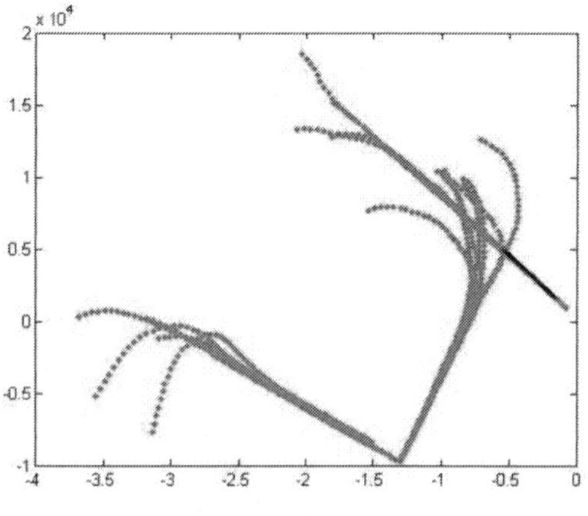

a

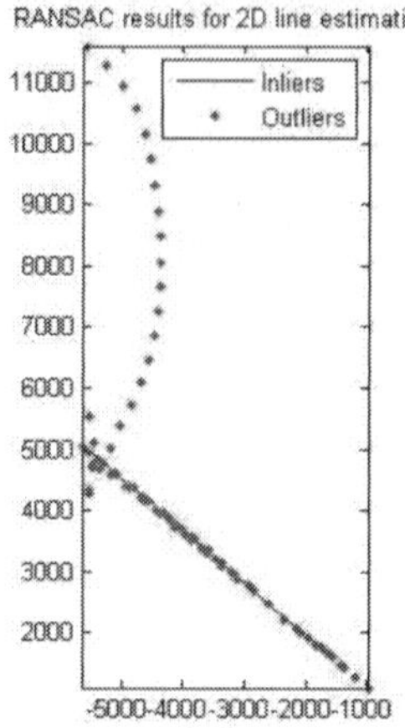

b

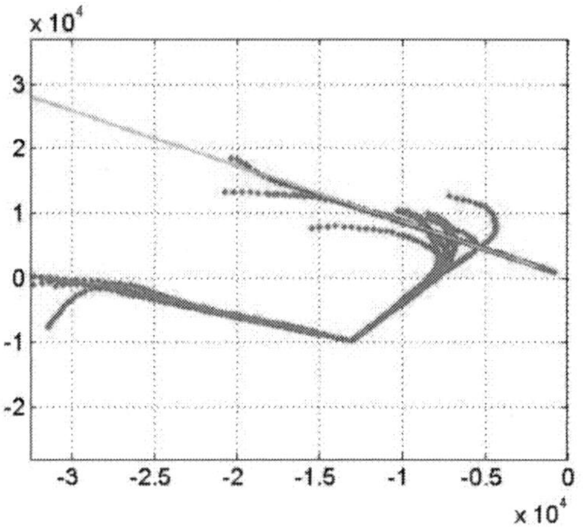

c

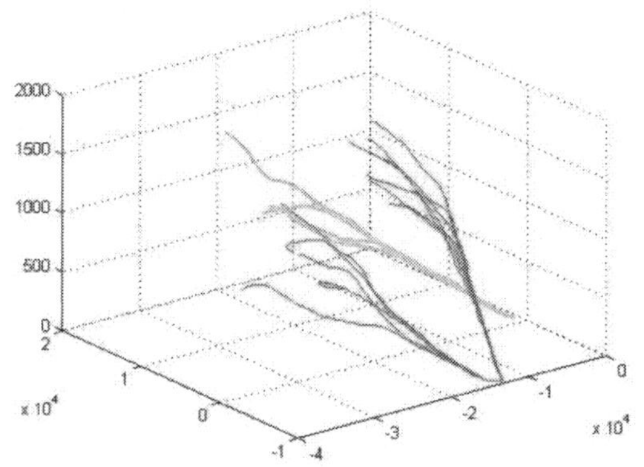

d

Fig.3. Results obtained at different stages of the algorithm are presented. a) Two-dimensional projection of scattered data (aligned with time); b) Linear regression of analysed scattered data obtained with RANSAC [8] algorithm; c) Asymptote (long blue line) of the first separated trajectory beam; d) Three finally separated trajectory beams in original 3D-space. The beam shown in blue corresponds to the asymptote represented in Fig.3c.

Conclusions

New data mining technique for analysis of multidimensional trajectories of landing aircrafts in 3D, described in the work, allows to obtain stable results in partitioning of the analyzed trajectory sample into asymptotically converged beams of the trajectories. Thus, 3D airspace sectorization of extended airport area may be performed.

DOI: 10.1051/itmconf/20160801001

References

1. A. McFadyen, T. Martin, M. O'Flynn, D. Campbell, *2016 IEEE Aerospace Conference* (IEEE, Big Sky, MT, 2016)
2. M. Sergeeva, D. Delahaye, C. Mancel, L. Zerrouki, N. Schede, *International Conference on Models and Technologies for Intelligent Transportation Systems* (IEEE, Budapest, 2015)
3. M. Gariel, A. Srivastava, E. Feron, *IEEE Transactions on Intelligent Transportation Systems* (IEEE, 2011) **12** (4), 1511-1524.
4. V. Bastani, L. Marcenaro, C. Regazzoni, *2014 IEEE International Workshop on Machine Learning for Signal Processing (MLSP)* (IEEE, 2014), p. 1-6
5. M. Enriquez, C. Kurcz, 5th *International Conferences on Research in Air Transportation (ICRAT)* (FAA, Berkley, Ca., 2012)
6. B. Kukharenko, M. Solntseva-Chalei, Informacionnye tehnologii **22** (2), p.83-89 (Novtech, Moscow, 2016)
7. B. Kukharenko, M. Solntseva, Informacionnye tehnologii (5), p.3-7 (Novtech, Moscow, 2014)
8. M. Fischler, R. Bolles, Communications of the ACM, **24** (6), p. 381-395 (1981)
9. P. Torr, A. Zisserman, Journal of Computer Vision and Image Understanding **78** (1), 138-156 (2000)
10. A. Dempster, N. Laird, and D. Rubin, Journal of the royal statistical society, p. 1-38 (1977)
11. I. Nabney, NETLAB: algorithms for pattern recognition. Springer Science & Business Media (2002).
12. S. Gaffney, P. Smyth, In Advances in neural information processing systems, p. 473-480 (2004)

The development of intermodal transport services on the basis of geoanalytical information

Denis Vlasov[1,*], *Anton* Menshutin[1], and *Nina* Danilina[2]

[1]Genplan Institute of Moscow, 125047, 2/14, 2-nd Brestskaya str., Moscow, Russia
[2] National Research University Moscow State University of Civil Engineering, 129337, 26, Yaroslavskoye Shosse, Moscow, Russia

Abstract. The article highlights the application of geoanalitical data for the purposes of urban transportation planning. It presents the original method for functional analysis and development of public transport transit hubs based on the study of cellular network information obtained from mobile operators, as a foundation for development of the effective intermodal system for public transportation services. The approbation of the suggested methodology was carried out using the results of analytical research of the data obtained from mobile network operators, serving the territory of Moscow. The results of research refer to one of the stations of the Moscow metro. Studying motion information of residents and workers provided by signal transmission from mobile communication network allows the authors to describe the area of major importance for the transit hub, needed to make valid design solutions at the stages of planning the effective work of the urban transport system.

1 Introduction

Effective management of a large metropolis represents an enormous challenge for the city government. The vastly diverse city assets are interconnected in most intricate ways. Changes applied to one part of the system can produce complicated results, having an effect on the entire city. In order to manage system that complex, a vast amount of data is required. Since a lot of such data essentially describes human behaviour, and because measuring human behaviour on a grand scale is very difficult, if not altogether impossible (at least within the realm of ethical and legal norms, and budgetary restrictions), an accessible proxy to direct behavioural metrics is often desired.
The sphere of public transportation services is among those most important city assets that do need such kind of information. The formation and development of convenient and safe system for intermodal transportation is an essential factor for sustained development of any settlement, especially the largest cities, agglomerations, conurbations and other contemporary forms of settlement. Intermodal transportation is understood by the authors as a well-developed system of passenger transportation, thus offering best possible

[*] Corresponding author: vlasych@mail.ru

coordination of different modes and comfortable transfer [1,2,3]. So, the main objective of this paper is to examine the possibility of implementation of geoanalytic data in urban planning studies. In particular, it is determining the prospects of intermodal transport infrastructure prosperity and the subsequent progress of "big data" processing methods on the simulation of the transport system development.

2 Methods

The critical issue for determining the prospects for the development of intermodal transport systems is that of valuation of traveler volumes along transit network, incoming and outgoing passengers for each transit hub. The affected area of a Transport Transit Hub (TTH) is a residential and/or employment area gravitating to it.

To date national urban development practices several analytical methods for calculating the areas affected by the Transport Transit Hub [4,5]:

- regulatory methods based on requirements on time or distance approach to TTH;
- graphic-analytical method of «isochrones» definition based on the speed analysis of major highways that ensure delivery of population to TTH;
- statistical method based on the analysis of load level of the ground public transport routes that ensure the delivery of the population to TTH.

The main disadvantages of the above methods are either small precision (the first and the second methods), or significant labor input (the third one). Therefore, there is a real need for the use of modern technologies for determining the area affected by one or another TTH [6,7]. Geoanalytical study of the obtainable data from cellular networks operators represents one of them.

Mobile phone operators collect a lot of technical data about operation of Base Transceiver Stations (BTS's) [8,9]. By analyzing this data, one can estimate, among other measurements, the total number of mobile devices at a given territory at different time spans, the number of trips between a pair of regions.

In this paper we show how mobile network data can serve as such a proxy. In particular, we describe how it can be used for the analysis and development of Moscow public transport transit hubs.

City occupies large portion of space and its infrastructure is very irregular in space. Thus, data that is required to describe the city should be spatial. Cellular networks collect device location data in order to provide service. Precision of this device location data varies with time and space. This data is collected at irregular time intervals. Events that trigger device location inquiry are either device specific or network specific. Device specific events are incoming or outgoing voice calls or SMS's, and device being switched on or off. Network specific events occur due to network related activity – crossing of Location area boundary or Periodic location update after extended period of inactivity. The frequency at which device location data is gathered is subject to exogenous factors and can't be influenced under normal course of operation since only passive collection is possible.

3 Implementation

In our study we use data on mobile network events in Moscow and Moscow region covering a period of one month. Total number of mobile devices covered by this study is approximately 20 million. For each event its date and time, cell and lac id, and device id were known. Coverage area for each cell was estimated, defined as locus of stable device-

to-cell linkage. Coverage area size may vary from few hundred meters to tens of kilometers, depending on the topography, building density, number of mobile subscribers within that area and types of devices they use, and some other factors. During the event the device location is recorded as particular cell coverage area.
In order to comply with privacy regulations, all data processing was implemented on cellular operator side. Data collection, algorithm implementation, and final processing were all carried by operator's IT team, thus preventing access to private data by the third party.
Data processing proceeded in three stages: pre-filtering, main processing, and data aggregation. Pre-filtering stage is straightforward: data from devices other that mobile phones (e.g. ATM, tablets, navigators, etc.) is removed. During the main processing stage, data is transformed from event-specific to location-specific. Since we are interested in the actual locations of devices and not in network events per se, chains of consecutive data entries generated by one device pointing to the same location were aggregated. Apart from obvious chains of events occurring within the same cell area, slightly more sophisticated filtering techniques were used, designed to detect situations where an unmoving mobile device registers cell change. This occurs e.g. when a device located near a border of two adjacent (or overlapping) coverage areas switches back and forth between those cells. This produces consecutive events where cell changes from, say cell #id1 to cell #id2 back and forth several times over a short period of time. If coverage areas of those cells overlap, then we assume that device is at a stop within that overlap area.

We next estimate place of residence and place of employment for each subscriber. Place of residence is defined as an area where subscriber spent most of the time during night hours through the month. Similarly, place of employment is defined as a location where subscriber spent most of the time during the working hours, and that is different from his place of residence. If those two locations match, than subscriber is assumed to be unemployed.

A mobile device that remained within the same area for 60 minutes or longer is assumed to be stationary for that period of time; we call that occurrence a static event. Device relocation occurs when the device moves from one cell area to another. A trip is defined as a consecutive sequence of device relocations, preceded and followed by two static events.

Trips that were made on metro were categorized into separate group. Technically it was possible as most of the metro network is underground, and id's of cells serving metro stations and tunnels are known. Therefore, with high probability, a subscriber entering the metro will register with a metro-serving cell, and will be dropped upon exiting metro. More complicated algorithms were utilized to account for above ground parts of metro, especially to identify trips that started or terminated at such stations.

From analytical perspective, separating metro trips from others is useful for two reasons. First, metro is the main mass-transit system in Moscow, the number of trips made on metro is high – almost 9 million during any given business day. Second, it allowed for additional verification of our transit estimates with metro-transit data.

Transformation of data to location-specific form and identification of trip-related events allows researcher to estimate variety of parameters that closely approximate behavior of people within the city, such as number of inhabitants residing within given region, number of trips between a given pair of regions, and so on.

4 Experiments

Data-aggregation stage served two purposes: one was to reduce the amount of data, the other was to preserve privacy. The choice of aggregation schemes depended on the specific topic of the report. Several reports on various topics were produced. Here are few examples of aggregation techniques. Let assume that place of employment and place of residence are known for each device. If we aggregate the database over the place of residence we can estimate the population of the given region. If we aggregate data over two columns we can estimate commute matrix.

a)
b)

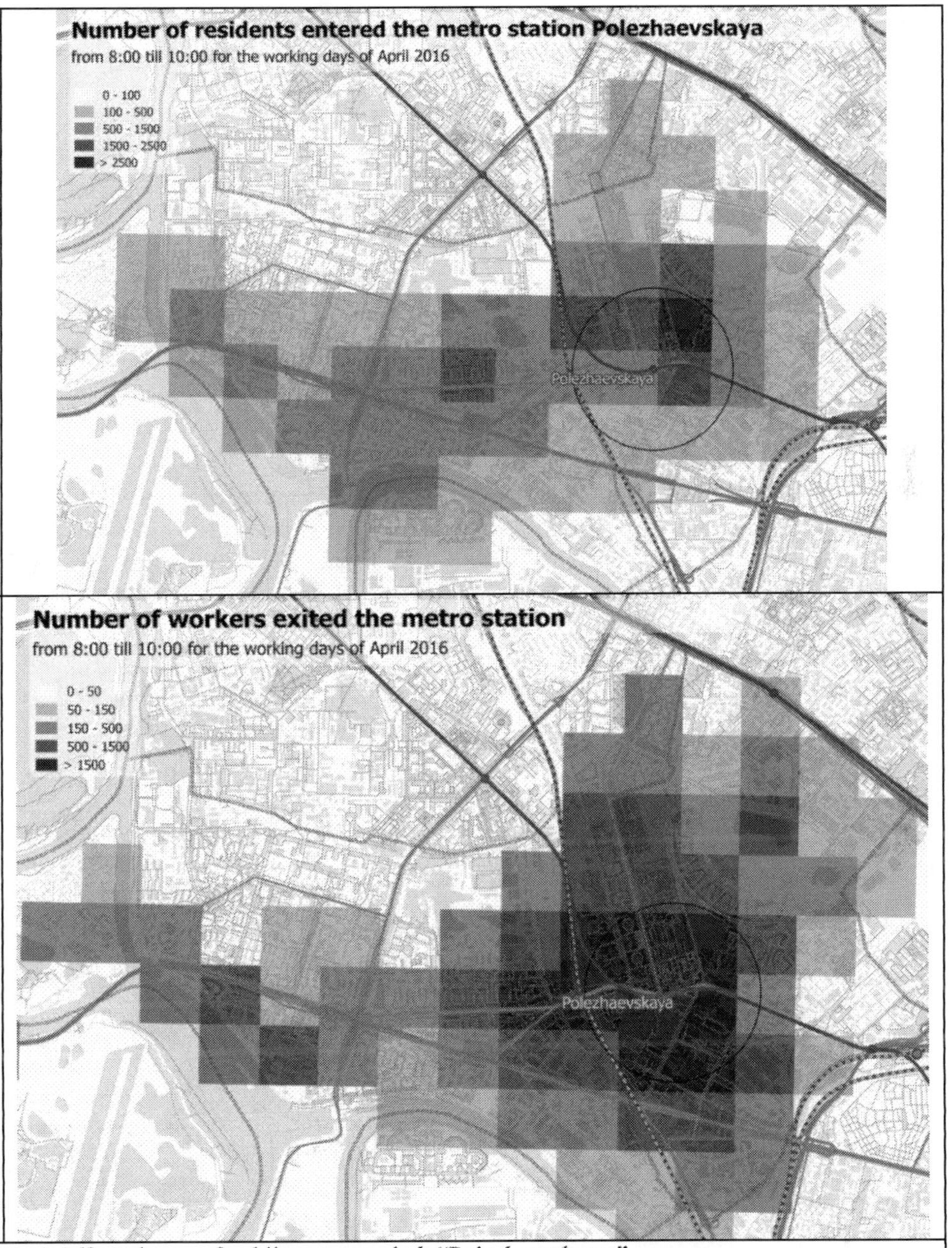

Figure 1 Affected area of public transport hub "Polezhaevskaya "
a) Residence affected area, b) Employment affected area

Transportation hubs analysis required aggregation of data to square grid of 500 by 500 meters cells. If a cell coverage area overlapped several grid cells, we randomly assigned its data to one of those grid cells, with probabilities proportional to intersection areas. In pre-aggregated form, data contained the following attributes for each trip made using Moscow metro:

1) Origin and destination metro stations.

2) Grid cell at which place of residence is located (if exists).
3) Grid cell at which place of employment is located (if exists).
4) Origin and destination grid cells.

The approbation of the suggested methodology was carried out for example at one of the stations of the Moscow metro at Tagansko-Krasnopresnenskaya line – station Polezhaevskaya, located at Moscow Northern administrative district. It is one of the busiest transport terminals enabling the number of linkages between land and off street transportation modes. Customers' access is provided by 7 bus and 6 trolleybus routes, as well as by private car and by foot. Objective of the research was to highlight the affected area of the TTH on the basis of the data of mobile operators on the use of station by residents and employees.

The results of the research at Polezhaevskaya Metro station are presented in Figure. 1, a,b.

The final aggregated report shows following attributes for each metro station:

1) Number of people residing within each grid cell.
2) Number of people being employed within each grid cell.
3) Number trips started from within each grid cell.
4) Number trips terminated at within each grid cell.

Frequency for all data is hourly. All estimates were done from 8 AM to 10 AM in work days, April 2016.

Our estimates show fairly good qualitative agreement when compared with results from population databases and transportation surveys: our estimates closely replicated dynamics of the real world data, namely periods of highest and lowest traffic loads (in both, metro and above ground transport). The quantitative agreement, however, wasn't as good: estimate error was usually within 10%-15% range. We attribute those discrepancies primarily to inaccuracies in location estimation.

5 Results

The research results reported in this article show that using a geoanalitical data offers the possibility to define the area affected by TTH and not only. It provides also unprecedented opportunities for analysis and studies in the other fields of urban transportation, such as:

- further justification for the classification provisions of transfer hubs to determine the priority directions for development of city transport system;
- TTH load forecast (which requires further research and identifying settlement patterns);
- various applied works, related to routings and frequencies of land public transport services basing, frequencies on off street high-speed lines and so on and so forth.

Development of methods related to data analysis of cellular operators, will significantly improve the accuracy of urban calculations and forecasts, provide municipalities with operational information on places of settlement and employment.

References

1. E. Sherbina, N. Danilina, D. Vlasov Int. J. of Appl.Engin. Res, **10**, pp 43131-43138 (2015)
2. D. Vlasov, N. Danilina *Public transport transit hubs system and "Park-and-Ride" facilities* Lap Lambert Publ., Germany, p. 81 (2013)

3. D. Vlasov *Transport transit hubs of big cities (on the Moscow example)*, M: ACB, p.96 (2009)
4. Bahirev I.A., Gradostroitel`stvo, **№ 2 (42),** pp. 12-19 (2016)
5. Mihailov A. YU., Kopylova T.A. Vestnik IrGTU **№ 7 (102)**, pp. 168-174 (2015)
6. K.Michael, B. Mccalla, E. Christine Geoforum, **43**, Iss.1, pp. 81–94 (2012)
7. Shilpa Shashikant Chaudhari, , Rajashekhar C. Biradar Journal of Network and Computer Appl., **72**, pp. 87–103 (2016)
8. YU. Tyan *Issledovanie metodov «big data» dlya prognozirovaniya parametrov transportnyh potokov*, report o NIR № Op-15-37-51307\15 ot 10.08.2015 (2015)
9. L. V. Lapidus Economica jeleznyh dorog, **11**, pp. 50-59 (2015)
10. A. Agafonov, A. Sergeev, A. Chernov Komp`uternaya optica, **36**, №3, pp.453-458 (2012)

ITM Web of Conferences **8**, 01003 (2016) DOI: 10.1051/itmconf/20160801003
ICBDA 2016

An Overview of Techniques for Cardiac Left Ventricle Segmentation on Short-Axis MRI

Arseny Krasnobaev[1*] and *Andrey* Sozykin[2]

[1]Krasovskii Institute of Mathematics and Mechanics, Yekaterinburg, Russia
[2]Ural Federal University, Yekaterinburg, Russia

Abstract. Nowadays, heart diseases are the leading cause of death. Left ventricle segmentation of a human heart in magnetic resonance images (MRI) is a crucial step in both cardiac diseases diagnostics and heart internal structure reconstruction. It allows estimating such important parameters as ejection faction, left ventricle myocardium mass, stroke volume, etc. In addition, left ventricle segmentation helps to construct the personalized heart computational models in order to conduct the numerical simulations. At present, the fully automated cardiac segmentation methods still do not meet the accuracy requirements. We present an overview of left ventricle segmentation algorithms on short-axis MRI. A wide variety of completely different approaches are used for cardiac segmentation, including machine learning, graph-based methods, deformable models, and low-level heuristics. The current state-of-the-art technique is a combination of deformable models with advanced machine learning methods, such as deep learning or Markov random fields. We expect that approaches based on deep belief networks are the most promising ones because the main training process of networks with this architecture can be performed on the unlabelled data. In order to improve the quality of left ventricle segmentation algorithms, we need more datasets with labelled cardiac MRI data in open access.

1 Introduction

Nowadays, heart diseases are the leading cause of death [1]. Non-invasive cardiac imaging technologies, such as magnetic resonance imaging (MRI), computerized tomography (CT), and echocardiography, are the essential tools for the diagnosis and treatment of such pathologies. In addition, with the help of these technologies the personalized heart models can be constructed in order to conduct the numerical simulations [2].

We present an overview of techniques for cardiac imaging segmentation, which is a delineation of heart chamber contours. The heart consists of four chambers, two ventricles and two atriums. Left ventricle (LV) is the biggest chamber of the heart and the most important one because it pumps blood to the entire body. Hence, in our review we are focused only on LV segmentation. Currently, the most precise source of information about the internal heart structure is the cine magnetic resonance imaging (MRI). We consider only the

* Corresponding author: arseny.krasnobaev@gmail.com

short-axis MRI view because it is more widely used than the long-axis one. In addition, LV shape on the short-axis slices is much simpler, than on the long-axis, hence, most of methods use only short-axis data.

Segmentation of LV is a crucial step for estimation of the important diagnostics indicators because accurate LV contours provide significant amount of information about its shape and size. Usually, a procedure is performed on a series of short-axis slice images taken at equal time intervals throughout one cardiac cycle (4D MRI data). This is a spatio-temporal pattern recognition task.

At present, LV segmentation is usually performed manually because the automated methods do not meet accuracy requirements. Every LV segmentation algorithm faces the same challenges caused by the LV anatomical structure. Trabeculations and the papillary muscles are located inside the LV cavity and are almost indistinguishable from the myocardium by intensity. Therefore, many different algorithms tend to suffer from the same issue of inner contours shrinking (Fig. 1). Another common problem is that the LV cavity region sometimes appears to be very small on apical and basal slices that leads to drastic imbalance between number of pixels belonging to the LV region and to the background. Finally, variability in shape and intensity of LV among patients can be significant, especially for pathological cases. Despite these obstacles, fully automated algorithms have progressed significantly in past two decades.

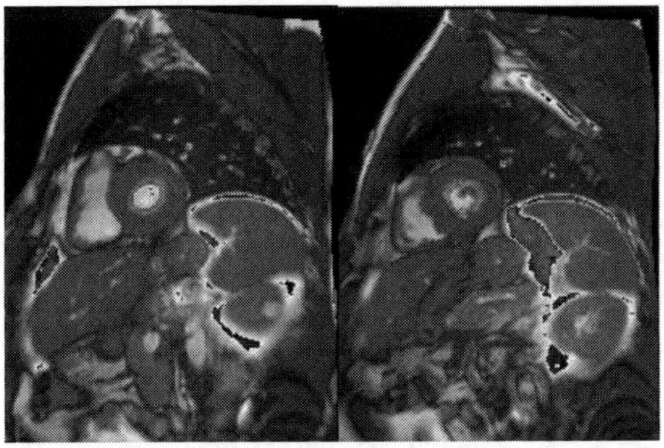

Fig. 1. The examples of LV segmentation on the short-axis MRI (left – accurate segmentation, right – LV contour shrinked due to the papillary muscles).

2 Segmentation Quality Evaluation

One of the critical tasks of choosing the appropriate LV segmentation techniques is to determine the accuracy of the algorithms. Most popular approaches are based on usage of metrics that compare contours produced by the algorithm with the ground truth segmentation. *Dice metric* (DM) is a measure of similarity between regions:

$$DM(S,M) = 2\frac{|S \cap M|}{|S|+|M|}, \quad (1)$$

where S is a detected region, M is a manually labelled one. DM is the main tool for LV detection accuracy evaluation because it is simple and relevant.

Jaccard index is close to DM, but preserves triangle inequality:

$$J(S,M) = \frac{|S \cap M|}{|S \cup M|} = \frac{DM(S,M)}{2-DM(S,M)} \quad (2)$$

 DOI: 10.1051/itmconf/20160801003

Hausdorff distance is another traditional approach to formalize the difference between regions in metric space:

$$d_H(S,M) = \max\left(\sup_{s\in S}\inf_{m\in M} d(s,m),\, \sup_{m\in M}\inf_{s\in S} d(s,m)\right) \quad (3)$$

In contrast to DM and Jaccard index, the Hausdorff distance considers metric distance between regions. Hence, it is sensitive to significant local shape deviations, but useless to detect continuous minor deviations like a contour bias. Therefore, DM and Hausdorff distance are complementary to each other and both of them should be used. The overall method reliability on a specific dataset can be formulated as a number of data items, on which quality metric exceeds some fixed threshold [3].

Finally, it is important to consider a specific dataset for quality evaluation, as image quality and anatomical deviations can greatly affect the results. There are a few cardiac MRI datasets publicly available:

• Sunnybrook Cardiac Data [4] was prepared for MICCAI (International Conference on Medical Image Computing and Computer Assisted Intervention) 2009 LV segmentation challenge. The dataset contains 4D MR images of 45 patients with ground truth contours of LV and myocardium. The dataset covers some anatomical pathologies.

• Kaggle Data Science Bowl Cardiac Challenge dataset includes short-axis MRI data for 700 persons. It is the biggest cardiac MRI dataset in an open access. Although the annotated contours are not provided, the dataset can be used for unsupervised learning.

• A dataset presented in the paper [5] provides short-axis MR images with annotated contours for 33 subjects.

3 Left Ventricle Segmentation Techniques

Although a large number of image segmentation algorithms has been developed, no universal solution suitable for every type of application is available. Hence, a wide variety of segmentation techniques has been developed specifically for various type of applications, including cardiac segmentation. Many completely different principles have been adopted, including heuristics and basic machine learning methods [6, 7], deep learning [8, 9], deformable models [10], and random forests [11]. Segmentation was even treated as a tracking problem and several complex statistical models have been proposed [12].

Despite the significant differences in the algorithms, a number of general steps are common for most of the approaches. These steps form a kind of a framework for cardiac structure segmentation [13]. Usually, the first step is a *pre-processing*, such as noise removal and intensity standardization. Next, the *region of interest* (ROI) detection is performed. Since the short-axis slices contain not only the heart itself, but also a whole thorax, it is reasonable to separate ROI that includes the heart and minimum of unrelated pixels. This step improves both performance and accuracy of further segmentation. The best way to separate ROI is to use the fact that the heart is the only area that changes significantly within one cardiac cycle. There are several ways to do it, for instance, thresholding pixels by a standard deviation of their intensities over the time on middle slice [7]. Another approach [6] involves Fourier transform to compute the first harmonic, it uses not only the fact of changing intensity, but also its fundamental frequency. For supervised methods, above-mentioned steps are also applied for training data.

After pre-processing the segmentation is performed. Semi-automated approaches can include limited user interactions, i.e. selecting a point inside the LV cavity.

3.1 Deep Learning

Convolutional neural networks (CNN) are deep artificial neural networks with a number of convolutional and subsampling layers [14]. Such architecture allows obtaining high node efficiency and reduces degree of freedom that lowers requirements for a number of training examples [15]. CNNs has become a preferred tool for general purpose 2D pattern recognition. Apparently, pure convolutional networks are rarely used for LV segmentation. A straightforward way is to train the deep network on ground truth contours to classify pixels [17]. Competitive results were declared, despite that only 2D segmentation was performed without using spatio-temporal relations among images.

Deep belief networks (DBN) are recently developed neural networks architecture. In contrast to CNN, DBN consists of fully connected layers, and the training process completely differs from the traditional backpropagation [16]. The training process is composed from two main stages. The first stage is an unsupervised pre-training of network treated as a stacked Restricted Boltzmann Machine, which is intended to learn unlabelled structure of data. The next step is a supervised stage of fine-tuning networks parameters with respect to labelled data with backpropagation. Such approach allows reaching high accuracy when a large amount of unlabelled data available to learn structure from, but only a small part of data is labelled. That makes DBN highly beneficial to real world applications. A recent research [9] has found an efficient way to combine DBN with level set method to attain a great endocardium segmentation quality.

3.2 Random Decision Forest

Random decision forest is a supervised regression and a classification machine learning method, known for its high generalizing ability and ease to train. Traditionally, the random forest is implemented by averaging results of a large number of decision trees, each of which is overfitted to perfectly recognize random subsampling or subspace of the original dataset. Such approach, called bootstrap aggregation, helps to overcome high predisposition of decision trees to overfitting and preserves high accuracy at the same time. Random forests are well-established for classification tasks, but relatively rarely used to image patter recognition. Nevertheless, a recent research has applied the combination of two forests for full spatio-temporal LV reconstruction using both the short-axis and long-axis view cine MRI images [11]. The approach uses one random forest for pre-processing (intensity standardization and orientation normalization) and another one for segmentation itself, with almost no other auxiliary processing. The relatively simple algorithm provides good results on the clear samples of interior slices. However, segmentation quality suffers on the apical and basal slices.

3.3 Deformable Models

Deformable models is a specific tool for image segmentation, based on the idea of iteratively evolving a curve or surface in order to minimize some functional [18]. An active contour model is a special case of deformable models, inspired by physics. This approach uses energy functional that is composed from image gradient throughout the curve evolved and contours tolerance for tension and bend. A level-set method is an implicit variation of the active contour model, which allows applying optimization directly to pixel grid, without necessity to parametrize a contour curve. The problem of active contour model is that all the terms required for object segmentation should be embedded into the energy function. Hence, to design such function manually is quite a challenging task. The contours that fitted to optimize simple gradient-based energy function tend to shrink inward or leak outward because such energy function reaches its minimum when it is on the ROI boundary. The problem can be solved by embedding into the energy function some prior information about LV shape, which can be obtained from another machine learning model. For instance, the energy can be regularized by the distance from the deformable contour to one retrieved by other approach, as described in [9]. Several recent researches, which declared state-of-art results (average DM value of 0.9-0.95), used combination of deformable models with another machine learning algorithms, such as DBN [9], CNN [8], or Markov random fields [10].

A combination of complex heuristics and deformable model, described in [19], preforms not as good as aforementioned combinations with advanced machine learning, yet it is quite competitive with DM value 0.91 on Sunnybrook dataset.

3.4 Graph-based Methods

According to the well-known image segmentation approach, which is based on max-flow problem solving, the image is treated as a graph. The nodes correspond to the pixels and the edges – to the pixel neighbourhood relations. The nodes are weighted with probability a_i of corresponding to foreground, b_i of corresponding to foreground and edges are weighted with $p_{i,j}$, which is a separation penalty. The goal is to find a partition of a pixel set into two sets, corresponding to background and foreground respectively by maximizing the functional:

$$q(A,B) = \sum_{i \in A} a_i + \sum_{i \in B} b_i - \sum_{i \in A, j \in B} p_{i,j} \tag{4}$$

The functional $q(A,B)$ is maximized by graph minimum cut, hence, the problem is reduced to finding max-flow/min-cut. A more general, but similar approach was used for LV segmentation [3] and reached DM of greater than 0.9 for LV cavity and 0.8 for myocardium segmentation.

3.5 Basic Machine Learning and Heuristics

Usually, the LV cavity is clearly distinguishable from the cardiac muscles on interior slices of short-axis MRI by intensity, thus it is possible to achieve the competitive results with only basic image segmentation algorithms and heuristics. Such approaches benefit from low requirements for computational power, which make them suitable for implementation in low-power hardware. Recent research [6] has proposed a stack of efficient heuristics, which accurately segments most of the interior slices. Since segmentation is based on intensity thresholding, algorithm is prone to fail on the cluttered slices, but in most cases, it provides satisfactory results.

Another paper [7] relies on principle of component analysis over a number of hand-coded per-pixel features like gradient magnitude, intensity and median filter value, and k-nearest neighbours algorithm for pixel classification. The satisfying results were declared on a small private dataset.

4 Conclusion

Comparing the LV segmentation algorithms is a challenging task because published segmentation results was obtained in diverse conditions on different datasets using various quality metrics. The most popular among them are the Sunnybrook Cardiac Data and the dice metric (Table 1). Although most of the algorithms work well on the mid-ventricular slices, the quality of apical and basal slices segmentation still needs further improvements.

Table 1. Comparison of LV cavity segmentation accuracy on the Sunnybrook cardiac data.

Method	Average dice metric
CNN and deformable models [8]	0.93
DBN and deformable models [9]	0.90
Heuristics and deformable models [19]	0.91
CNN standalone [17]	0.86

The current state-of-the-art approach is a combination of the deformable models with the advanced machine learning techniques, such as deep learning or Markov random fields. Such algorithms are being actively researched; the papers [8-10] declared segmentation accuracy comprising average dice metric value of 0.9+ for inner and outer contours of LV on Sunnybrook dataset. We expect that DBN-based approaches are the most promising ones because the main training process of DBN can be performed on the unlabeled data.

Further development of segmentation techniques is impeded by the lack of training data. In order to develop the high quality fully automated LV segmentation algorithms we need more datasets with labelled MRI data in open access. In addition, the common approach to evaluation of cardiac segmentation algorithms quality is required.

This work was supported by the Russian Science Foundation (grant no. 14-35-00005).

References

1. D. Mozaffarian et al., *Heart Disease and Stroke Statistics – 2016 Update*. American Heart Association (2016)
2. S.F. Pravdin, V.I. Berdyshev, A.V. Panfilov, L.B. Katsnelson, O.E. Solovyova, V.S. Markhasin. *Mathematical model of the anatomy and fibre orientation field of the left ventricle of the heart.* Biomedical engineering online. 12:**54** (2013)
3. I.B. Ayed, H. Chen, K. Punithakumar, I. Ross, Sh. Li, *Max-flow segmentation of the left ventricle by recovering subject-specific distributions via a bound of the Bhattacharyya measure*, Med. Image Anal., **16**, (2012)
4. P. Radau, Y. Lu, K. Connelly, .G Paul, A.J. Dick, G.A. Wright. *Evaluation Framework for Algorithms Segmenting Short Axis Cardiac MRI.* The MIDAS Journal – Cardiac MR Left Ventricle Segmentation Challenge, http://hdl.handle.net/10380/3070, (2009)
5. A. Andreopoulos, K. John, *Efficient and generalizable statistical models of shape and appearance for analysis of cardiac MRI*, Med. Image Anal., **12**(3), pp. 335-357, (2008)
6. X. Lin, B. Cowan, A. Young, *Automated Detection of Left Ventricle in 4D MR Images: Experience from a Large Study*, LNCS, **4190**, pp. 728-735, (2006).
7. M.M.A. Hadhoud, M.I. Eladawy, A. Farag, F.M. Montevecchi, U. Morbiducci, *Left Ventricle Segmentation in Cardiac MRI Images*, American Journal of Biomedical Engineering, **2**(3), pp. 131-135, (2012)
8. M. R. Avendi, A. Kheradvar, H. Jafarkhani, *A Combined Deep-Learning and Deformable-Model Approach to Fully Automatic Segmentation of the Left Ventricle in Cardiac MRI,* Med. Image Anal., **30**, pp. 108–119, (2016).
9. T. A. Ngo, G. Carneiro, *Left ventricle segmentation from cardiac MRI combining level set methods with deep belief networks,* 2013 20th IEEE International Conference on Image Processing (ICIP), pp. 695-699, (2013)
10. L. Cordero-Grande, G. Vegas-Sánchez-Ferrero, P. Casaseca-de-la-Higuera, J. A. San-Román-Calvar, A. Revilla-Orodea, M. Martín-Fernández, C. Alberola-López,

Unsupervised 4D myocardium segmentation with a Markov Random Field based deformable model, Med. Image Anal. **15**(3), pp. 283–301, (2011)
11. J. Margeta, E. Geremia, A. Criminisi, N. Ayache, *Layered spatio-temporal forests for left ventricle segmentation from 4D cardiac MRI data*, LNCS, **7085**, pp. 109-119, (2011)
12. W. Sun, M. Cetin, R. Chan, V. Reddy, G. Holmvang, V. Chandar, A. Willsky, *Segmenting and Tracking the Left Ventricle by Learning the Dynamics in Cardiac Images*, LNCS, **3565**, pp. 553-565, (2005)
13. T.N. Shewaye, *Cardiac MR Image Segmentation Techniques: an overview*, http://arxiv.org/pdf/1502.04252.pdf (2015)
14. L. Yann, B. Yoshua. *Convolutional Networks for Images, Speech, and Time Series*, The Handbook of Brain Theory and Neural Networks, MIT Press, pp. 1344, (1998)
15. M Lai, *Deep Learning for Medical Image Segmentation*, https://arxiv.org/pdf/1505.02000.pdf (2015)
16. G. E. Hinton, S. Osindero, Y.W. Teh, *A fast learning algorithm for deep belief nets,* Neural computation, **18**(7), pp. 1527–1554, (2006)
17. P. V. Tran, *A Fully Convolutional Neural Network for Cardiac Segmentation in Short-Axis MRI*, http://arxiv.org/pdf/1604.00494.pdf (2016)
18. T. McInerney, D. Terzopoulos, D*eformable Models in Medical Image Analysis: A Survey*, Med. Image Anal. **1**(2), pp. 91–108 (1996)
19. H. Hu,Z. Gao,L. Liu,H. Liu,j. Gao, et al. *Automatic Segmentation of the Left Ventricle in Cardiac MRI Using Local Binary Fitting Model and Dynamic Programming Techniques.* PLoS ONE **9**(12) (2014)

Study of The Correlation Between World Patenting Trends and The University Admission Rate in Russia Based on Open Data

Igor Balk[1]*, *Elena* Tishchenko, *Natalia* Ivashchenko[1]
[1]Lomonosov Moscow State University

Abstract. This paper discusses use of the open PCT patent data and university admission rate to study world technological trends and correlation between industry trends and the student admission rate for government sponsored University programs in Russia. OECD open statistical database and Lomonosov Moscow State University open admission data is used as a data source in this study. ICT and biotechnology industries used as a sample industries to study this correlations.

Keywords: open data, ITC, biotechnology, patent trends, admission rate, government scholarship in Russia

1 Patens as a data source of the technological trends monitoring

It is well know that number of issued patent can be used as economic indicator to monitor industry trends. According to the study conducted by NSF on the Science Indicators and Engineering in 2012, it is possible to show relationship between the number of conducted research works and the number of patents filed (the country's leaders are the same). [1] At the same time, according to the World Patent Organization, there is a definite correlation between the number of patents registered in the territory of the country and its gross domestic product (GDP). So Russia from 1997 to 2011 doubled its GDP, at the same time doubled and the number of registered patents (see. Figure 1-3) [2].

In the study "Using patent data for technology analyses and planning" Mary Ellen Mogee notes that patents have several advantages as a "technology indicator" [3]. It is important to note that the average ratio between the number of patents and the number of jobs in the computer manufacturing industry is 55.5 patents per year for 1,000 jobs in the chemical industry is already 16 patents per year for 1,000 jobs in the production of plastic 10, 2 patents for 1,000 jobs, and in the food industry 0.1 patents per year for 1,000 jobs. On average in the US economy 1,000 jobs produces 25.5 patent for 5 years or 5.1 patents per year [4].

* Corresponding author email info@innoationlabs.net

DOI: 10.1051/itmconf/20160801004

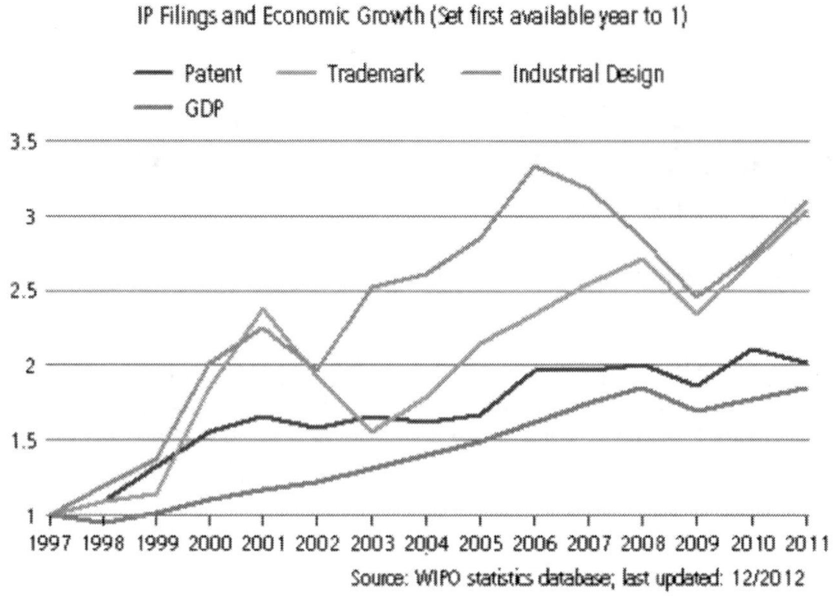

Fig. 1. GDP ratio, the number of applications for invention patents / trademarks / industrial designs in Russia [2].

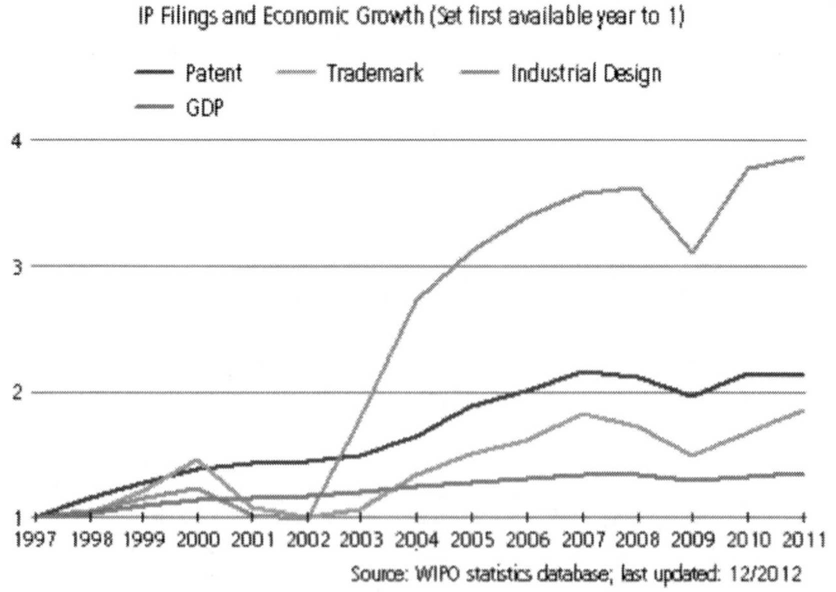

Fig. 2. GDP ratio, the number of applications for invention patents / trademarks / industrial designs in the US [2].

DOI: 10.1051/itmconf/20160801004

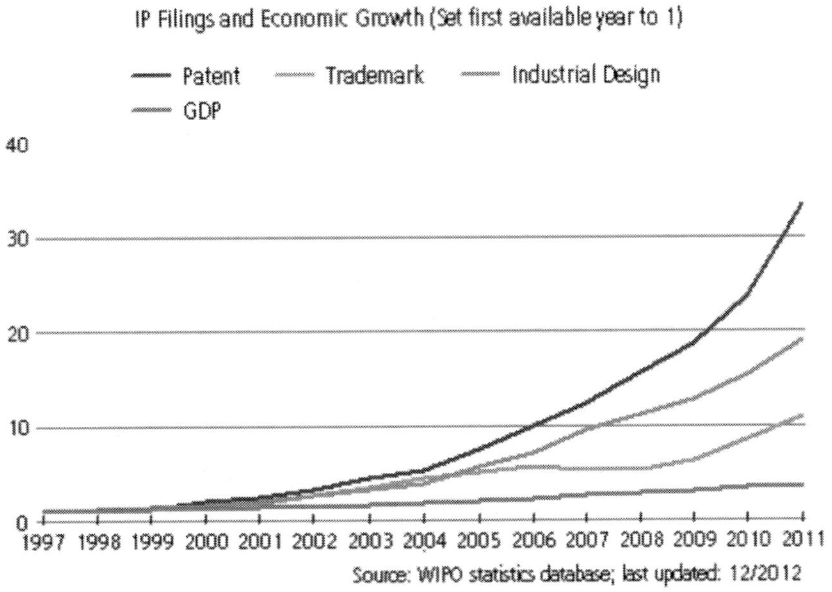

Fig. 3. GDP ratio, the number of applications for invention patents / trademarks / industrial designs in China [2].

2 Methodology of the study

The number of patents filling in the world in close to several hundred thousand with number of issued patents close to two hundred thousand each ear. The most challenging part is to create common ontology of the patent subject matter so it would be possible to relate patent data to the specific industries and skillsets. Another challenge was that there is no well-defined API neither for WPO nor for more commonly used Google Patent database.

The main goal of this study was to find if there is a correlation between world industry trends, Russian industry trends and the admission rate to the Russian universities. For this study we have selected two most dynamic in terms of patent filings industries – information technologies and biotechnologies. As a benchmark Russian university we have selected Lomonosov Moscow State University (MSU) which is according to the QS and THE world university ranking system is the best Russian university and one of the best universities in BRICs countries.

For the purpose of this study we have combined admission rates [6] at the government sponsored scholarships to departments of Mechanics and Mathematics, Applied Mathematics and Cybernetics and Physics as a benchmark for information technology and departments of Bioengineering and Bioinformatics, Biology, and Chemistry as a benchmark for biotechnologies.

For the patent data we used open OECD statistical databases [5] and we used only PCT issued patent data as it gives better representation of the real technological trends in the industry than national applications.

3 Findings

In this paper we will use described approach to consider date from OECD statistics database and correlate it to the official admission statistics of Lomonosov Moscow State University. We normalized all the data using data for 1999 as a reference. As we can see from the Figure 4 Russia and the rest of the world have significantly accelerated number of PCT filings while EU and USA filings are relatively flat. From this figure we can also see the tool which world economic crisis of 2001 and 2008 took on the number of PCT filings. What is interesting that admission rate to the ICT related departments of Lomonosov Moscow State University shows inverse correlation with economic crisis we can see that it picket around 2001 and 2008. It

DOI: 10.1051/itmconf/20160801004

is also shows inverse correlation with the EU and the US patent trends demonstrating that Russian government doing a good job managing number of government scholarships in the ICT field and it could be related to the exponential grows of the Russian PCT filings.

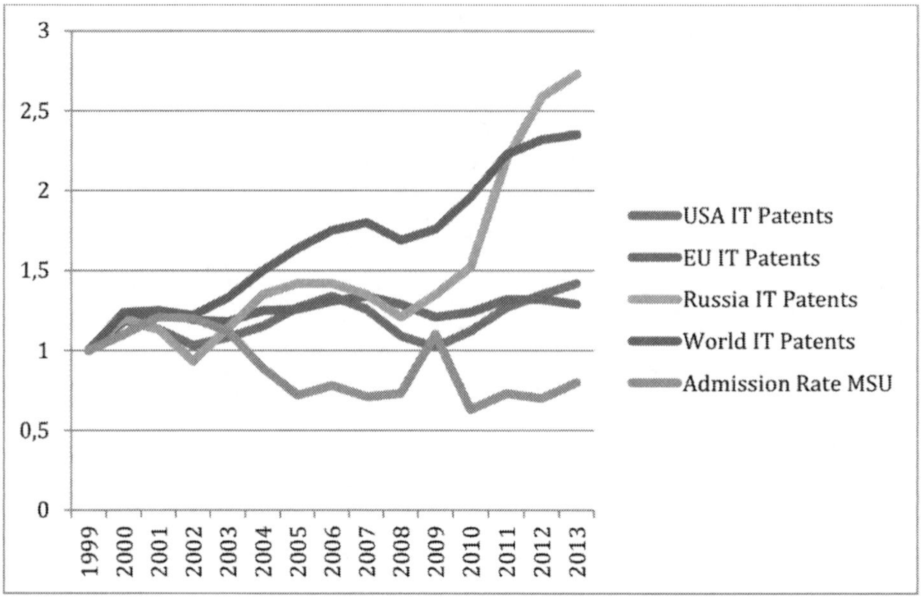

Fig. 4. Normalized number PCT (in the ICT related fields) patents filed by year and normalized admission rate to the corresponding departments of MSU.

We used the same approach to study correlation between the admission rate to the government-sponsored programs and technology trends in biotech field (Figure 5). As can be seen from the graph there is a correlation between number of Russian PCT filings in the biotech field and the admission rate. What is more interesting that we can see that spike in the admission rate flattered out and started to track average number of PCT patents around 2010. It could be attributed to better management of prospective students expectation or better management of government sponsored programs after the economic crisis of 2008-2009.

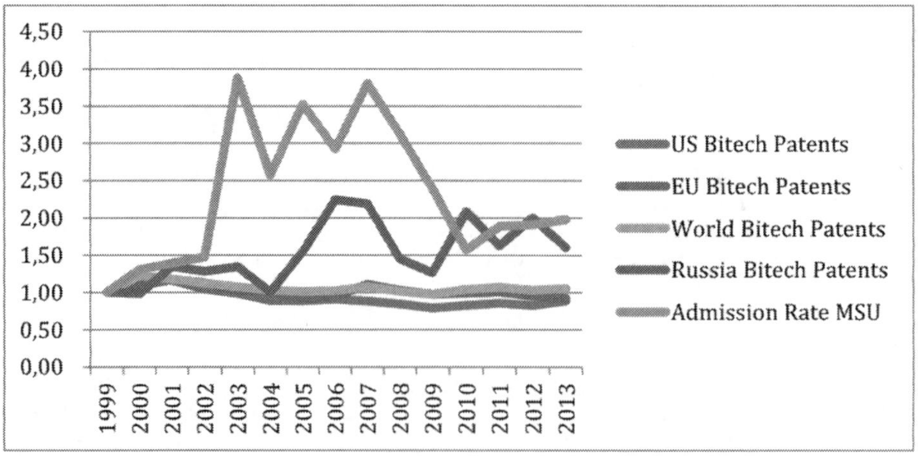

Fig. 5. Normalized number PCT (in the biotechnology related fields) patents filed by year and normalized admission rate to the corresponding departments of MSU.

4 Conclusions

As we can see from the study there is a correlation between technological trends and the admission rate to the Russian government sponsored programs at Lomonosov Moscow State University both in ICT and biotechnological fields. Further study is required to find the reason why ICT field shows invers correlation while biotechnological field demonstrates a direct one. This study is important part of the treatment effect study of the government programs on innovation economy conducted by authors [7].

References

1. WPO statistics http://www.wipo.int/ipstats/en/statistics/country_profile/
2. Science and Engineering Indicators 2012 Arlington, VA (NSB 12-01), January 2012 http://www.nsf.gov/statistics/seind12/c4/c4h.htm#s2
3. Mary Ellen Mogee, Using Patent Data for Technology Analysis and Planning, Research-Technology Management Vol. 34 , Iss. 4,1991
4. US PTO IP Report March 2012 http://www.uspto.gov/news/publications/IP_Report_March_2012.pdf
5. OECD open access statistical data http://www.oecd.org/sti/inno/oecdpatentdatabases.htm
6. Lomonosov Moscow State University statistics http://www.msu.ru/entrance/concurs.html.
7. Igor Balk, Egor Mateshuk Cluster analysis of the bias in the SMB subsidy recipients selection 6th Seminar on Industrial Control Systems: analysis, modeling and computation Moscow February 2016 DOI: 10.1051/itmconf/20160602002

ITM Web of Conferences **8**, 01005 (2016) DOI: 10.1051/itmconf/20160801005
ICBDA 2016

Analysis Of Multidimensional Data With High Dimensionality: Data Access Problems And Possible Solutions

Andrey Borodin[1,*], *Sergey* Mirvoda[1] , and *Sergey* Porshnev[1]

[1] Department of Radio Electronics for Information Systems, Ural Federal University, Russia

Abstract. This article covers the problem of access to multidimensional data with the dimension of 10^4 order. It contains the description of the system and the problem revealed in the process of its building, as well as engineering solutions applied to solve the similar problems. It is also clarified, why such solutions cannot be used for the treatment of the problem concerned. The existing engineering solutions are specified so that it is possible to presuppose the prospects of use of the fragments of such technologies for solving the problem in question.

1 Introduction

Nowadays, multidimensional data structures [1,2] are used in the information-processing systems (IPS) applied in the various fields of human activities, such as the business analysis [3], astronomy [4], geomatics [5], bioinformatics [6], etc. The analysis of their use shows that the rate of multidimensional data access is one of the main factors that influence the operation speed of the IPS. That is why, the development of rapid multidimensional data access algorithms is a highly topical problem. By now, over 30 years [2] have passed after the start of development (the 80-s of the last century) of the algorithms for the general solution of the problem concerned, but despite certain results achieved in this field, no universal automated algorithms adaptable to any specific multidimensional data structure have been developed yet. As a consequence, an IPS cannot be built using the available multidimensional data access technologies without their material updating or creating new algorithms adapted to the peculiarities of the information being collected and processed at a certain production facility.

The authors faced the similar situation when implementing, with a participation of a Russian institution of higher education, a complex project for the development of a high-tech production called "Development of an Automated System for Tracking, Control, Modeling, Analysis, and Optimization of the Full Cycle of Metallurgical Production based on the Creation and Integration of Mathematical Models of Technological, Logistic, and Business Processes of the Production Facility (Automated System for Metallurgical Production, MP AS)" (Code number 2012-218-03-167). MP AS consists of two interrelated modules: the automated information system for collection and analysis of the data of the

* Corresponding author: amborodin@acm.org

DOI: 10.1051/itmconf/20160801005

production facility (DCA AIS) and the automated information system for the simulation of the technological, logistic, and organizational (business) processes of the production facility (ODM AIS).

The initial information analysis revealed that the structure of data collected and processed by the DCA AIS under development is characterized by a big number of heterogeneous dimensions (the list of measurable process variables, including the online ones, comprises over 7000 names), for which the corresponding data can be retrieved. At the same time, the data characterizing the metallurgical production technological processes are highly integrated and cannot be divided between the different program modules.

One of the possible solutions of the said problem, proved to be reasonable by the experiments undertaken at the stage of the rough design of MP AS with the test data, is based on the use of the fastest up-to-date server hardware and software. Yet, its practical realization would evidently result in the sharp rise of the project cost. Moreover, we cannot be sure that the selected computational capabilities would be sufficient to ensure the required performance of execution of the data warehouse (DW) queries after the long-term operation of the system and accumulation of the big volume of data in the DW. The described situation proves the urgent need to develop the algorithms providing the fast access to heterogeneous multidimensional data of high dimensionality (the data with the total number of dimensions of 10^4 and more).

This article contains the general formulation of the problem concerning the access to multidimensional data with high dimensionality, the results of the analysis of the possibility to apply the available multidimensional data access methods, including the bitmaps, spatial hashing, multiple index connection method, as well as the suggested approach ensuring the fast access to multidimensional data with high dimensionality.

2 Problems of Access to Multidimensional Data with High Dimensionality

Each analytical system is purposed for making certain computations using the respective data. In the process of computations, computation resources are consumed, which are used for solving the two quasi-independent problems: access to the data stored in the DW and handling the extracted data.

This fact can be illustrated by the simple examples given below.

Example 1. There is a Microsoft Excel table containing the columns respectively called *A*, *B*, and *C*. The C column contains values calculated by the formula: $C = A + B$. Thus, the operation can be presented as an abstract syntax tree that consists of one node corresponding to the operation of addition (data handling), and the process of obtaining values from the specific cells of *A* and *B* columns can be considered as the data access.

Example 2. Building the three-dimensional scene on the monitor screen. In this case, the handling of data (mostly, computation of matrix products) is the most costly operation in terms of the use of computation resources. At the same time, the data retrieval requires much less computation resources than the data handling, as the volume of the initial data used in the computations is comparably small.

Example 3. Finding the way in the meeting graph of a large social network linking two and/or more users. In this case, the computations are made with a minimum amount of arithmetic or conditional operations, but due to the big volume of initial data and (typically) the use of the distributed data storage method, significant computation resources are required to access such data.

Historically, solving the problems of the specialized access to multidimensional data has been closely connected with the memory hierarchy. The term "hierarchy" itself also has a historical nature. In general, this is about the way of ranking the types of computer memories: from the fast, size-limited, and expensive memory (processor registers, cash, RAM) to the slow and cheap memory (hard disk systems, reservation systems, cloud storages). The key aspect of most multidimensional data access methods is lowering the number of queries to the slow memory due to the efficient layout of data in the fast memory.

It is characteristic of the multidimensional data access that the data search (a query) usually refers to several different data properties (different dimensions) at the same time. In this case, the list of the data properties used in the search query is known in advance. However, their number is usually so large, that it is almost impossible to build all one-dimensional search structures for all dimension combinations. For example, a query (that should be efficient in terms of the resource utilization) to a multidimensional data structure containing the anthropometric information about a large number of people, purposed to find the people having the nose length, the height, the birth date falling within the specified intervals. Here, the intervals setting the required values for the nose length, the height, and the birth date serve as the search criteria, whereas the information fields containing the values of the nose lengths, heights, and birth dates of the people included in the database (DB), are the active dimensions of the search query. A database may have a number of different dimensions, but a multidimensional data structure should ensure the equal efficiency of all queries made to it, regardless of the combination of available active dimensions used in the respective query.

Below are given the examples of information systems, where multidimensional information is being processed.

Example 4. Geographic information systems. Although these IPS traditionally operate with 3 to 4 dimensions (3 spatial coordinates and the time), they are also referred to the class of information systems with the multidimensional data processing. This is conditioned by the high variability of the queries used in such systems, e.g. "the search of the houses within the given rectangle", "the search of the gas stations nearest to the car location", or "the search of the best route with three or more changes", etc.

Example 5. Business analysis systems. Such IPS handle the data using dozens of search dimensions [7]. For example, a query of a business analysis system may look as follows: calculate the total income from all operations performed under the certain group of tariffs, within the certain date ranges, in the certain district of the city, for the subscribers having the connection to the digital TV and the broadband Internet access.

Today, there exist a great number of various data structures; some of them are described in [8]. Most of today's data structures represent the subset of the so called generalized index search tree (GiST) [9], formed by way of division of the whole data space into the hierarchically nested groups being the nodes of the tree. The grouping of objects in the indexed data space is performed so that the number of groups affected by the most probable data queries is reduced to a minimum.

A data access structure is selected based on the structure of the data and the query. The so called search query efficiency models are used to substantiate the selection of a specific balanced tree structure in quantitative terms. For example, in [10] it is offered to estimate the efficiency of the spatial indices used for making queries to the business analysis multidimensional data using the following model:

$$p(|q|,|s|)=\frac{|s|+|q|}{(1-|q|)(1-|s|)},$$

$$W(0,|s|)=|s|,$$

$$W(x+1,|s|)=\frac{\sqrt[D]{F}-1}{\sqrt[D]{N(x)}}+W(x,|s|).$$

$$DA=1+\sum_{x=1}^{\lceil\log_F N\rceil}\frac{N}{F^x}\prod_{j=1}^{D}p\left(W\left(x,|s_j|\right),|q_j|\right),$$

Fig. 1. The Model for making queries to the business analysis multidimensional data

where *DA* (disk access) is a number of the analyzed nodes of the tree data index;
N is a number of indexed records;
F (fanout) is a branching ratio of the tree index;
p(s,q) is a probability of intersection of *s* and q ranges;
W(x,s) is an average data range for one dimension grouped *x* times;
D is an indexed data dimensionality;
s is an average range occupied by one element of the initial data.

Moreover, as specified in [10], in the general case when we deal with the business analysis data with the number of dimensions of 10^1 order, the complexity of computation of the fixed result query (the number of data meeting the query criteria) — the ratio between *DA* and the size of the resulting sample has the complexity O(*N* log *N*). However, at larger *D* values (e.g, those of 10^4 order), $\sqrt[D]{F}\approx 1$ and $W(x+1,|s|)\approx W(x,|s|)$ it means that the interlevel data grouping is inefficient due to the reduction of range of the analyzed tree nodes when going down the index tree. As a result, the complexity of the fixed result query computation turns out to be O(*N*).

3 Problems of Bitmap Indexing of Multidimensional Data with High Dimensionality

The bitmap indexing method [11] (the bitmap method), as compared to the method of balanced trees, makes it possible to realize a simpler, as regards the computations, technology of organization of the quick search of data by multidimensional conditions. This technology is based on the ideas used in the binary computation facilities. Under the bitmap indexing method, each possible element of the data dimension is correlated with a bitmap, which is filled in with zeroes or ones depending on the consistency or inconsistency of values of the fields of all DB rows to the query field values. The sequence of the bitmap completion repeats the sequence of the DB data fields retrieved for the query. The search of the rows meeting the conditions of the conjunctive query is performed by the bitmaps multiplication. After that, the ones remaining in the obtained product correspond to the numbers of the rows meeting a condition of the multidimensional query. The technology is proved to be efficient; it is utilized in most up-to-date DBMS.

The technology allows to efficiently determine the identifying information of the data rows. However, the data access problem has not been yet fully solved in it, as after finding the rows meeting the query conditions, it is necessary to obtain the values of the attributes of the retrieved rows using the identifying information (lookup operation). In terms of the

DBMS terminology, this means that a bitmap is a noncluster index. For the physical retrieval of multidimensional data, a Gilbert codes arrangement is used, e.g. in Microsoft Analysis Services, as follows from the comments posted by one of the authors of this method in his blog [12]. At the same time, the study [13] contains the examples, where such method appears to be inefficient for the work with the high dimensional data.

The problem arising when using lookup operations for the computation of the multidimensional data query can be illustrated by the following example. Let us assume that we have N rows with D dimensions, each of which possesses on average M possible values. This information should be arranged in the data blocks of F rows, so that each query with one condition (the total number of possible variants — D·M) would require the use of a minimum possible number of information blocks DA, which should be referred to when obtaining access to the data meeting the query conditions. However, when $D>>F$, it is impossible to minimize DA, if D dimensions include no interrelated ones; in other words, the grouping of the data rows under one attribute results in the serious deviations of another attribute.

It should be noted, that most of available spatial indexing methods are based, inter alia, on the interrelation between the dimensions. Spatial indices can use certain local dependencies detected in the certain data subsets considered as nonlinear ones. We believe that nonlinear relations (e.g., between the groups of dimensions) can also be effectively used when applying the bitmap indexing method for the high dimension data access.

4 Spatial Hashing Method

The locality-sensitive hashing method (LSH) [6]) is worth mentioning, as it is successfully applied in the different fields of information technologies [14] dealing with multidimensional data of high dimensionality. The key idea of the method implies that a hash code coinciding with high probability is generated for the spatial points located close to each other.

There are three basic ways of using LSH method to access the data:

1. To generate a hash code for the query and the data row, so that one hash code corresponds to one query. All records meeting the query conditions should have the same hash code.
2. To generate a hash code, so that a set (in most cases — a multidimensional range (parallellotope)) of hash codes corresponds to one query. Accordingly, the records meeting the conditions of such query should have one of the possible hash codes, i.e. a point of multidimensional space belonging to the parallelotope.
3. To generate a hash code, so that one hash code corresponds to one query. In such a case, the considered hash code is assigned to most records meeting the conditions of such multidimensional query.

The first of the described data access methods is actually a one-dimensional method, as different combinations of dimensions would require different hash functions. The second method, in case of the growth in the number of dimensions, is prone to the ''combinatorial explosion" of the parallelotope volume. Consequently, their efficiency is below the efficiency of other available methods of multidimensional data access.

The third method cannot ensure the correct result of the query execution.

5 Method of Multidimensional Indices Junction

One of the most popular engineering practices used in relational databases when solving this problem is building a specific index for each dimension. During the execution of a multidimensional query, RDBMS joins the results of filtration of the separate conditions by the corresponding indices.

The simplicity of programming and reliability (in terms of reduction of probability of logical errors in the algorithms for the multidimensional query computation) are the obvious advantages of the suggested structure of a cluster index of a one-table multidimensional data warehouse. It is also noteworthy that the efficiency of the said index is independent of the number of dimensions in the indexed data. At the same time, it is probable that such indicator would be rather dependent on the number of dimensions stated in the query conditions. In fact, the data access system would need to compute all samples for the separate query conditions, each of which can appear much bigger than the sample corresponding to the conjunction of the query conditions.

6 Conclusion

The above analysis of the existing methods for the organization of the data access for the computation of multidimensional queries in the systems with a number of independent data dimensions of 10^4 order has revealed that neither of them can be deemed a universal instrument for solving the considered problem. Thus, there is a real need in the development of new problem-solving approaches. We deem it promising to apply the method based on the use of the hybrid technology integrating one or more of the above mentioned multidimensional data access methods. Such technologies have already proved their efficiency in solving the problems of access to multidimensional data with a number of dimensions of 10^0-10^2 order— for example, a so called BR-tree [15] with a Bloom bit filter inserted in its nodes [16].

The advantage of the bitmaps, which can be used in the hybrid method, is the absence of the explicit dependence of the query computation efficiency on the number of the indexed data dimensions, that is why they are used when solving the problems of 10^4-dimensional data indexing. Above that, when spatial indices are used, it is possible to use local nonlinear dependencies between the dimensions. We believe that the combination of these technologies would allow to create the system for analyzing the multidimensional data with high dimensionality, where the time needed to obtain the computation results would be measured in dozens of milliseconds rather than dozens of minutes.

References

1. V. Gaede. Multidimensional Access Methods / Gaede V., Gunther O. // ACM Computer Surveys. 1998. Vol.30. No. 2. P. 170-231.
2. D. Greene. An Implementation and Performance Analysis of Spatial Data Access Methods/ Greene, D. // In Proceedings of the Fifth IEEE International Conference on Data Engineering. 1989. P. 606-615.
3. A. M. Borodin, S. V. Porshnev, M. A. Sidorov. Application of Spatial Indices for the Processing of Analytical Retrievals and Aggregation of Multidimensional Data in IAS. Tomsk Polytechnical University Publishing. 2008 No 5, Pp. 64-86.
4. M. Frialis. Data Management and Mining in Astrophysical Databases // PhD thesis, Univ. of Udine, Italy. 2005.
5. K. T. Chang. Introduction to Geographical Information Systems/ K. T. Chang // New York: McGraw Hill.-2008. P. 184.
6. A. Andoni. Near-Optimal Hashing Algorithms for Approximate Nearest Neighbor in High Dimensions / Alexandr Andoni and Piotr Indyk // Communications of the ACM. Vol. 51. No. 1. 2008. P. 117-122.

DOI: 10.1051/itmconf/20160801005

7. A. M. Borodin, S. V. Porshnev. Comparative Analysis of the Possibilities and the Rate of Processing of Multidimensional Data by the Business Analysis Software Based on the Main Memory Indexing Structures. Scientific and Technical News of SPbGU. Series ''Computer Science, Telecommunication, Management" -2010. –No. 1. Pp. 99-102.
8. V. K. Gulakov, A. O. Trubakov. Multidimensional Data Structures. 2010. Bryansk: BSU Publishing, P. 387.
9. J. Hellerstein. Generalized Search Trees for Database Systems /J. Hellerstein, J.Naughton, A. Pfeffer// Proc. 21st Int'l Conf. on Very Large Data Bases. Zurich. September, 1995. P. 562-573.
10. A. M. Borodin, S. V. Porshnev. Analytical Methods for Estimating the Efficiency of Spatial Indices Application in OLAP Systems. [Text]. Scientific and Technical News of SPbGU. Series ''Computer Science, Telecommunication, Management" -2011. Pp. 93-100.
11. T. Johnson. Performance Measurements of Compressed Bitmap Indices / Johnson T.// - Proceedings of 25th International Conference on Very Large Data Bases. September 7-10, 1999. P. 278-289.
12. M. Posumanskiy. Chronicle Number 9 "We Are Great Minds". [Digital resource] // URL : http://web.archive.org/web/20040306084024/http://www.mosha.com/XRONIKI/win-xronika9.html (access date 10/13/2013)
13. A. M. Borodin, S. V. Porshnev. Algorithms for the Quick Access to Multidimensional Data in OLAP Systems. Saarbrucken: LAP Lambert Academic Publishing. 2012. P. 176
14. A. Rajaraman. Mining of Massive Datasets, Ch. 3. /A. Rajaraman, J. Ullman // Stanford University, California, 2010. P. 326.
15. Yu Hua. BR-Tree: A Scalable Prototype for Supporting Multiple Queries of Multidimensional Data /Yu Hua , Bin Xiao, Jianping Wang // Computers, IEEE Transactions on. Vol. 58. Issue 12. 2009. P. 1585-1598.
16. B. H. Bloom. Space/time trade-offs in hash coding with allowable errors/ Burton H. Bloom // Communications of the ACM T. 13 (7). 1970. P. 422-426.

ITM Web of Conferences **8**, 01006 (2016) DOI: 10.1051/itmconf/20160801006
ICBDA 2016

Learning Word Subsumption Projections for the Russian Language

Dmitry Ustalov[1,2,*], *Alexander* Panchenko[3]

[1]Krasovskii Institute of Mathematics and Mechanics, 620990 Yekaterinburg, Russia
[2]Ural Federal University, 620002 Yekaterinburg, Russia
[3]Technische Universität Darmstadt, Computer Science Department, Language Technology Group, 64289 Darmstadt, Germany

Abstract. The semantic relations of hypernymy and hyponymy are widely used in various natural language processing tasks for modelling the subsumptions in common sense reasoning. Since the popularisation of the distributional semantics, a significant attention is paid to applying word embeddings for inducing the relations between words. In this paper, we show our preliminary results on adopting the projection learning technique for computing hypernyms from hyponyms using word embeddings. We also conduct a series of experiments on the Russian language and release the open source software for learning hyponym-hypernym projections using both CPUs and GPUs, implemented with the TensorFlow machine learning framework.

1 Introduction

In Linguistics, hyponymy denotes the asymmetric relationship between a generic term (hypernym) and a specific instance of this term (hyponym). These relations are similar to the relations between genus and species in Biology and called "subsumptions". For instance, the word "cat" is a hyponym of the word "feline". Traditionally, dictionaries of hypernyms and hyponyms are created manually by expert lexicographers or extracted automatically using lexico-syntactic patterns from a large collection of documents [1].

Since the inception of efficient methods for computing low dimensional word embeddings by Mikolov et al. [2], a significant attention has been paid to how distributional semantics can model relations of specific types, such as hypernyms or synonyms. One way to specify the type of relations between word vectors, investigated in this paper, is to induce a matrix such that multiplying on which a hyponym vector provides a hypernym vector. In particular, we investigate such an approach in the context of the Russian language.

In this paper, we will briefly review the related studies in Section 2 and describe the approach learning word subsumptions in Section 3, providing the open source implementation. We also conduct the performance study along with the quality evaluation in Section 4. Then, we discuss the obtained results in Section 5. Finally, we conclude with final remarks in Section 6.

* Corresponding author: dau@imm.uran.ru

2 Related Work

Currently, the most widely used method for detecting hypernyms and hyponyms is the Hearst patterns [1]. These lexical-syntactic patterns, e.g., "*Y such as X_1 and X_2*", have successfully found a substantial number of applications including ontology learning [3]. However, these patterns offer an inconvenient to work with the sparse representation of words which is being nowadays addressed using the word embeddings [2].

Fu et al. [4] proposed the projection learning approach to learning hypernyms for the Chinese language. This approach assumes learning the projection matrix such that multiplying on which a hyponym vector provides a hypernym vector. The learning problem has been posed as the linear regression problem that has been then numerically approximated using stochastic gradient descent. Also, the k-means clustering algorithm has been used to split the embeddings space to several subspaces to provide more flexibility to the model.

Levy et al. [5] observed the lexical memorization effect when using hyponym and hypernym embeddings for subsumption classification task. However, they conclude that it is still possible to learn "prototypical hypernyms", i.e., the word categories, due to the reported effect.

Kutuzov et al. [6] showed that the word embeddings can serve as informative language-independent semantic fingerprints when exploited in the problem of multilingual text clustering. In particular, the projection learning method similar to the one presented in our paper was used to translate words from Russian to Ukrainian, trained on a bilingual dictionary.

The method of Kutuzov et al. mentioned above stems from the original publication of Mikolov et al. [7], where projection learning was used to translate words from English to Spanish. More recently, Vulic et al. [8] presented a systematic study of four classes of methods for learning bilingual embeddings. The authors find approach based on linear projection, similar to the one we use in our method, to be most practical and efficient.

Vylomova et al. [9] evaluated several popular approaches for computing semantic relations and found that in word embeddings, vector subtraction generalises well to a broad range of relations, including over unseen lexical items.

Shwartz et al. developed an integrated method that combines the syntactic parsing features with word embeddings based on a long short-term memory network [10]. The resulting method called HypeNET has been implemented using the recurrent neural network that encodes the patterns with the embeddings.

3 Method

In the baseline setting proposed by Fu et al. [4], the projection matrix is obtained similarly to the linear regression problem, i.e., for the given row vectors $\mathbf{x}$ and $\mathbf{y}$ representing the hyponym and hypernym embeddings correspondingly, the $|\mathbf{x}| \times |\mathbf{y}|$ matrix Φ^* is numerically approximated:

$$\Phi^* = \arg\min_{\Phi} 1 / N \sum_{(\mathbf{x},\, \mathbf{y})} \mathrm{dist}(\mathbf{x}\Phi, \mathbf{y}), \quad (1)$$

where N is the number of training examples and $\mathrm{dist}(\mathbf{x}\Phi, \mathbf{y})$ is the distance between a pair of row vectors $\mathbf{x}\Phi$ and $\mathbf{y}$. In the original method, the Euclidean distance (L^2 distance) is used. However, in distributional semantics, the cosine distance and similarity are the more widely used measures [2], so it is reasonable to study their performance. The distributed word representations tend to promote synonyms and other related words among the hypernyms [11], which are of the primary interest. Thus, it seems also reasonable to provide the examples of undesired relations to refine the matrix being approximated.

3.1 Variations

Here, we propose three variations to the above-mentioned method: hyponymy penalization, synonymy penalization, and hypernymy promotion. Each variation consists of modifying the loss function by introducing the additional term weighted by the constant α or β that control the balance between two components of the loss function (in our experiments we used $\alpha = 0.01$ and $\beta = 0.3$. For preventing the difference from being negative, we use the absolute value.

3.1.1 Hyponymy Penalization

Our first variation is designed for enforcing the asymmetry of the projection matrix given the fact the subsumption is an asymmetric relation. Thus, applying the same transformation to the hypernym vector $\mathbf{x}\Phi$ as to the hyponym vector should not provide the initial hyponym vector $\mathbf{x}$.

$$\Phi^* = \arg\min_\Phi 1 / N \left|(1-\alpha) \textstyle\sum_{(\mathbf{x},\mathbf{y})} \mathrm{dist}(\mathbf{x}\Phi, \mathbf{y}) - \alpha \textstyle\sum_{\mathbf{x}} \mathrm{dist}(\mathbf{x}\Phi\Phi, \mathbf{x})\right| \qquad (2)$$

3.1.2 Synonymy Penalization

Our second variation introduces the approach of negative sampling, i.e., explicitly providing the examples of synonyms $\mathbf{z}$ that penalizes the matrix to produce the vectors similar to them.

$$\Phi^* = \arg\min_\Phi 1 / N \left|(1-\alpha) \textstyle\sum_{(\mathbf{x},\mathbf{y})} \mathrm{dist}(\mathbf{x}\Phi, \mathbf{y}) - \alpha \textstyle\sum_{(\mathbf{x},\mathbf{z})} \mathrm{dist}(\mathbf{x}\Phi\Phi, \mathbf{z})\right| \qquad (3)$$

The main obstacle to realizing this loss function is the introduction of the $\mathbf{z}$ term representing a synonym of the given word $\mathbf{x}$, because certain words might have no synonyms. In such cases, we substitute $\mathbf{z}$ with $\mathbf{x}$, gracefully reducing to the previous variation. Otherwise, on each batch, we sample a random synonym of the given word.

3.1.3 Hypernymy Promotion

Our third variation is designed for promoting the projection matrix to produce hypernyms not just for the initial hyponym, but also for its randomly sampled synonym $\mathbf{z}$. This is motivated by the fact that in lexical ontologies the words are grouped into synsets (sets of synonyms) and the subsumptions are established between such synsets. So, both hyponym and its synonym are supposed to have the same hypernym.

$$\Phi^* = \arg\min_\Phi 1 / N \left[(1-\beta) \textstyle\sum_{(\mathbf{x},\mathbf{y})} \mathrm{dist}(\mathbf{x}\Phi, \mathbf{y}) + \beta \textstyle\sum_{(\mathbf{x},\mathbf{z})} \mathrm{dist}(\mathbf{z}\Phi, \mathbf{y})\right] \qquad (4)$$

In the case of no synonyms available, i.e., $\mathbf{x} = \mathbf{z}$, this variation gracefully reduces to the baseline setting.

3.2 Implementation

Instead of the linear regression used to approach this problem [4], our implementation is based on the single-layer perceptron developed using the TensorFlow open source framework for machine learning [12] that supports both CPU and GPU computation of the numerical optimization procedures. Particularly, each input hyponym embedding x has been provided with an additional bias dimension. Thus, a vector $\mathbf{x}' = (1, \mathbf{x}_1, \ldots, \mathbf{x}_{|\mathbf{x}|})$ has been used instead of the original vector. Similarly, the projection matrix is now $|\mathbf{x}'| \times |\mathbf{y}|$. For minimizing the loss functions, we use the Adam stochastic optimization method [13]. We provide both implementations for L^2 and cosine distances for the loss functions, but our evaluation is focused only on the former due to the poor preliminary performance results of the latter.

4 Experiments

In our experiments, we use the following openly available language resources for Russian:

- pre-trained word embeddings in the form of 500-dimensional vectors computed using the skip-gram architecture [2] having the context window parameter as 10 words with the minimum word frequency of 5 (this model has been among the best ones in the RUSSE evaluation campaign [14]);
- a set of subsumption pairs obtained automatically using Hearst patterns from a large text corpus [14, 15];
- a set of subsumption pairs and synonyms derived from the Russian Wiktionary [16].

Particularly, as it has been suggested in [5], we split the train and test sets such that each contains a distinct vocabulary to avoid the lexical overfitting of the models. As the result, the training set contains 21 997 examples, the test set contains 10 811 examples. The test set contains only the examples from Wiktionary, while the training set is composed of other sources as well. We ran 14 000 training epochs; each passes a batch of 512 examples to the optimizer. The dimensions of the projection matrix are 501×500. At the initialization stage, we initialize the elements the projection matrix with N(0, 0.1). In the experiments, we study the performance of the loss functions operating with the L^2 distance along with the benefit of the clustering.

Since that the specificity of the relations differs in various regions of the embedding space, we employed the same clustering algorithm as described in [4, Section 3.3.2]. Initially, we estimated the number of clusters by maximizing the Silhouette score [17], but this approach led us to the suboptimal number of clusters $k = 2$. Instead, we evaluated all the values of $1 \leq k \leq 10$ to find the optimum on the test set. Each experiment has been run for five times to make it possible to assess the statistical significance of the results using the one-tailed t-test with the significance level of 0.025.

4.1 Quality Evaluation

In order to assess the quality of the model, we employed the following technique. For each subsumption pair $(\mathbf{x}, \mathbf{y})$ of hyponym $\mathbf{x}$ and the related hypernym $\mathbf{y}$ in the test set, we selected the projection matrix Φ_k^* assigned to the same cluster k as the given pair. Then, we compute ten nearest neighbours for the projected hypernym. The pair is considered matched if the word representing the gold hypernym $\mathbf{y}$ appears in the computed list of the nearest neighbours $\mathrm{NN}_{10}(\mathbf{x}\Phi_k^*)$. In order to obtain the integrated quality score, we average the matches across the test set:

$$\mathrm{A@10} = 1 / N \sum_{(\mathbf{x},\mathbf{y})} \mathbb{1}(\mathrm{NN}_{10}(\mathbf{x}\Phi_k^*) \ni \mathbf{y}), \quad (5)$$

where N is the number of test examples and $\mathbb{1}(\,)$ is the indicator function. Intuitively, the A@10 measure is the probability of providing the correct hypernym among the ten nearest neighbours by projecting its related hyponym, which is previously unknown to the model.

Since the list of the nearest neighbours of the non-transformed hyponym vector may also contain hypernyms [11], it yields A@10 = 0.0877 on our test set.

4.2 Performance Study

Since that TensorFlow has been used for defining and executing the computation graph, we paid attention to the comparison of the CPU and GPU performance in our task. Therefore, for our experiments, we used the following computational resources available on a single machine:

- Intel Xeon E5-2620 v2 @ 2.10GHz (32 GB of RAM), denoted as CPU;
- NVIDIA Tesla K20Xm, 2866 cores (6 GB of VRAM), denoted as GPU.

5 Results and Discussion

According to the evaluation results in Table 1, both our variations implying penalizing the hyponymy and synonymy statistically significantly outperform the baseline in most settings. However, hypernymy promotion, inspired by lexical ontologies, showed the results worse than the baseline. Thus, we conclude that such a penalization can provide the system with the useful lexical information. Interestingly, no variation performed better than the baseline on $k = 6$ due to the inconsistent clustering.

Table 1. Quality evaluation according to A@10,
the best statistically significant result compared to the baseline in each setting is highlighted.

Model	k=1	k=2	k=3	k=4	k=5	k=6	k=7	k=8	k=9	k=10
Baseline	.1407	.2141	.2563	.2652	.3037	.3101	.3156	.3168	.3530	.3394
Pen. Hyponymy	**.1428**	.2161	.2591	.2700	.3100	.3080	.3255	.3268	.3655	**.3528**
Pen. Synonymy	.1427	**.2169**	**.2599**	**.2704**	**.3110**	.3093	**.3258**	**.3271**	**.3673**	.3526
Pro. Hypernymy	.1366	.2087	.2519	.2619	.3019	.3078	.3148	.3147	.3551	.3418

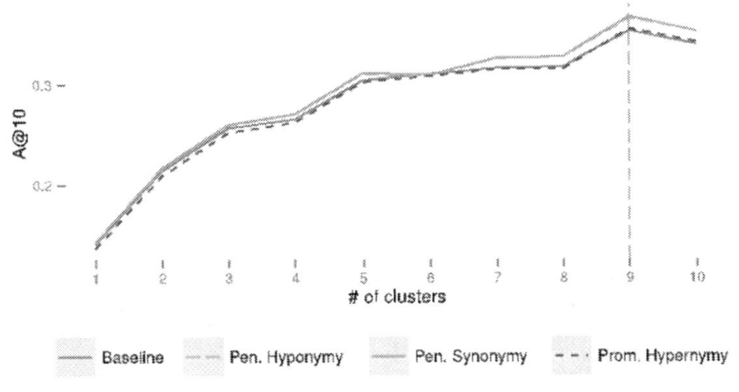

Fig. 1. Evaluation results according to the A@10 measure, the best result on all the variations is achieved on $k = 9$.

Increasing the number of clusters seems to be an efficient mean for increasing the capacity of the machine learning model. However, we found that the results stopped improving after $k = 9$, suggesting extending the training and test set sizes (Fig. 1). Since that the clustering reduces the number of the train items available per cluster, we had to use a relatively low batch size. To study the performance of the training procedure w.r.t. the

DOI: 10.1051/itmconf/20160801006

batch size, we run 1000 training epochs for the batch sizes of 512, 1024, 2048, 4096 and 8192. Table 2 shows the results of the performance study, confirming that under the present settings using a GPU makes the training process slower (Fig. 2) due also to the matrix size.

Table 2. Performance study: the total number of seconds spent per 1K training epochs on various batch sizes.

Model	Device	512	1024	2048	4096	8192
Baseline	CPU	1.52	2.05	3.18	7.61	14.38
Pen. Hyponymy	CPU	2.23	3.21	5.57	13.01	24.09
Pen. Synonymy	CPU	2.24	3.24	5.54	13.07	24.05
Pro. Hypernymy	CPU	1.77	2.64	4.59	10.87	20.47
Baseline	GPU	1.83	2.35	3.75	6.81	13.10
Pen. Hyponymy	GPU	2.39	2.95	4.39	8.00	13.92
Pen. Synonymy	GPU	2.57	3.22	4.99	8.87	15.98
Pro. Hypernymy	GPU	2.30	3.08	4.82	8.85	14.99

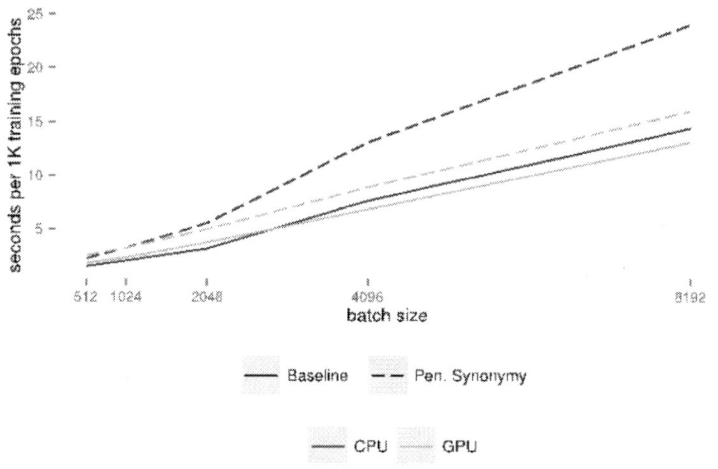

Fig. 2. Performance study of the baseline approach and the synonymy penalization approach involving negative sampling.

We also conducted a series of experiments with the cosine distance instead of the L^2 distance, but virtually in all the settings the A@10 measure was one and half times worse than using the L^2 distance, while the training process took ten times longer time. During these experiments, we removed the absolute value bars and replaced the negative distance terms in the equations (2) and (3) with the positive values of cosine similarity, making the loss function still non-negative.

6 Conclusion

In this study, we developed three models for learning word subsumptions and evaluated them on several resources for the Russian language. We also presented the open source software implementing the described approach, which is available under the terms of a libré license: https://github.com/dustalov/projlearn. Our datasets are available for other studies: http://ustalov.imm.uran.ru/pub/projlearn-ruwikt.tar.gz. To the best of our knowledge, this is the first study dedicated to learning subsumptions using word embeddings for the Russian language.

In the further studies, we are interested in applying convolution layers for capturing high-level features of word embeddings, increasing the number of neural network layers, and using the learned matrices to construct semantic hierarchies. We also plan to conduct a crowdsourcing experiment to compare our results with the human judgements in order to weaken the dependency from the gold standard.

The reported study was funded by RFBR according to the research project No. 16-37-00354 мол_а. We are grateful to Nikolay Arefyev, Andrey Kutuzov, Andrey Krizhanovsky, Benjamin Milde and Alexander Bersenev for the fruitful discussions on the present study. Dmitry Ustalov was partially supported by the Deutscher Akademischer Austauschdienst (DAAD) scholarship. Alexander Panchenko was supported by the Deutsche Forschungsgemeinschaft (DFG) foundation under the project "JOIN-T: Joining Ontologies and Semantics Induced from Text".

References

1. M.A. Hearst. Automatic Acquisition of Hyponyms from Large Text Corpora. Proceedings of the 14th Conference on Computational Linguistics - Volume 2. COLING '92, Association for Computational Linguistics (1992) 539–545
2. T. Mikolov, I. Sutskever, K. Chen, G.S. Corrado, J. Dean. Distributed Representations of Words and Phrases and their Compositionality. Advances in Neural Information Processing Systems 26. Curran Associates, Inc. (2013) 3111–3119
3. A. Panchenko, S. Faralli, E. Ruppert, S. Remus, H. Naets, C. Fairon, S.P. Ponzetto, C. Biemann. TAXI at SemEval-2016 Task 13 a Taxonomy Induction Method based on Lexico-Syntactic Patterns, Substrings and Focused Crawling. Proceedings of the 10th International Workshop on Semantic Evaluation (SemEval-2016). (2016) 1320–1327
4. R. Fu, J. Guo, B. Qin, W. Che, H. Wang, T. Liu. Learning Semantic Hierarchies via Word Embeddings. Proceedings of the 52nd Annual Meeting of the Association for Computational Linguistics (Volume 1 Long Papers), Association for Computational Linguistics (2014) 1199–1209
5. O. Levy, S. Remus, C. Biemann, I. Dagan. Do Supervised Distributional Methods Really Learn Lexical Inference Relations? Proceedings of the 2015 Conference of the North American Chapter of the Association for Computational Linguistics Human Language Technologies, Denver, Colorado, Association for Computational Linguistics (2015) 970–976
6. A. Kutuzov, M. Kopotev, T. Sviridenko, L. Ivanova. Clustering Comparable Corpora of Russian and Ukrainian Academic Texts Word Embeddings and Semantic Fingerprints. Proceedings of the Ninth Workshop on Building and Using Comparable Corpora. (2016) 3–10
7. T. Mikolov, Q.V. Le, I. Sutskever. Exploiting Similarities among Languages for Machine Translation. CoRR abs/1309.4168 (2013)
8. I. Vulić, A. Korhonen. On the Role of Seed Lexicons in Learning Bilingual Word Embeddings. Proceedings of the 54th Annual Meeting of the Association for Computational Linguistics (Volume 1 Long Papers), Berlin, Germany, Association for Computational Linguistics (2016) 247–257
9. E. Vylomova, L. Rimell, T. Cohn, T. Baldwin. Take and Took, Gaggle and Goose, Book and Read Evaluating the Utility of Vector Differences for Lexical Relation Learning. Proceedings of the 54th Annual Meeting of the Association for Computational Linguistics (Volume 1 Long Papers), Berlin, Germany, Association for Computational Linguistics (2016) 1671–1682

10. V. Shwartz, Y. Goldberg, I. Dagan. Improving Hypernymy Detection with an Integrated Path-based and Distributional Method. Proceedings of the 54th Annual Meeting of the Association for Computational Linguistics (Volume 1 Long Papers), Berlin, Germany, Association for Computational Linguistics (2016) 2389–2398
11. A. Handler. An empirical study of semantic similarity in WordNet and Word2Vec. Master's thesis, University of New Orleans (2014)
12. M. Abadi et al. TensorFlow Large-Scale Machine Learning on Heterogeneous Distributed Systems. CoRR abs/1603.04467 (2016)
13. D.P. Kingma, J. Ba. Adam A Method for Stochastic Optimization. CoRR abs/1412.6980 (2014)
14. N. Arefyev, A. Panchenko, A. Lukanin, O. Lesota, P. Romanov. Evaluating Three Corpus-Based Semantic Similarity Systems for Russian. Computational Linguistics and Intellectual Technologies Papers from the Annual International Conference "Dialogue", Volume 2 of 2. Papers from special sessions, Moscow, RGGU (2015) 106–118
15. A. Panchenko, O. Morozova, H. Naets. A Semantic Similarity Measure Based on Lexico-Syntactic Patterns. Proceedings of KONVENS 2012, ÖGAI (2012) 174–178
16. A.A. Krizhanovsky, A.V. Smirnov. An approach to automated construction of a general-purpose lexical ontology based on Wiktionary. Journal of Computer and Systems Sciences International 52(2) (2013) 215–225
17. P.J. Rousseeuw. Silhouettes: A graphical aid to the interpretation and validation of cluster analysis. Journal of Computational and Applied Mathematics 20 (1987) 53–65

Planning of Autonomous Multi-agent Intersection

Ilya I. Viksnin[1,*] *Igor* A. Zikratov[1], *Andrei* A. Shlykov[1], *Daria* L. Belykh[2], *Igor* I. Komarov[1] and *Gennady* A. Botvin[2]

[1]ITMO University, Department of Secure Information Technology, Kronverkskiy pr., 49, Saint Petersburg, Russia, 197101
[2]SPbU, Department of Information Systems in Economy, Universitetskaya emb., 7/9, Saint Petersburg, Russia, 199034

Abstract. In this paper, we propose a traffic management system with agents acting on behalf autonomous vehicle at the crossroads. Alternatively to existing solutions based on usage of semiautonomous control systems with the control unit, proposed in this paper algorithm apply the principles of decentralized multi-agent control. Agents during their collaboration generate intersection plan and determinate the optimal order of road intersection for a given criterion based on the exchange of information about them and their environment. The paper contains optimization criteria for possible routes selection and experiments that perform in order to estimate the proposed model. Experiment results show that this model can significantly reduce traffic density compared to the traditional traffic management systems. Moreover, the proposed algorithm efficiency increases with road traffic density. Furthermore, the availability of control unit in the system significantly reduces the negative impact of possible failures and hacker attacks.

1 Introduction

One of the most significant current discussions in the automobile industry is about quickly developing technologies for robotic vehicle control. This is confirmed by the active participation of almost all the leading foreign automakers, many domestic and several research teams and companies in intelligent control system development in order to achieve driving without human control. Currently existing technical devices for vehicle control automation are considered as assistance to the driver in real road conditions when driver is dealing with individual management tasks. Such assistance systems contain a variety of Parking sensors and Parking Assistant, cruise control and autopilots, systems of emergency braking before the obstacle, etc. But current studies in this field are also aimed at the development of algorithms for automobile control for future when a person will not participate in the process of the unmanned vehicle control. [1]

It leads to developing new algorithms for autonomous vehicle control, which can handle a set of interrelated tasks[2-5]. These algorithms provide smooth car movement, correct

**Corresponding* author: wixnin@cit.ifmo.ru

DOI: 10.1051/itmconf/20160801007

route selection [6]. Also these algorithms make it possible to prevent collisions with obstacles [7] and other road users [8], organize safe and rapid intersection crossroad [9—13] and etc.

* *Corresponding* author: wixnin@cit.ifmo.ru

These algorithms are designed with two interrelated goals. The first one is increasing the efficiency of intersections. It can be achieved by using algorithms of optimal control during communication of autonomous vehicle network. The second one is providing road security. The security issues are resolved by eliminating human factor influence on the process of vehicle control and equipping drones and road infrastructure by the set of sensing devices, allowing real-time the traffic monitoring in various road and environmental conditions.

This paper organized as follows: Section 2 contains comparison of two different approaches for swarm robots control. In section 3 we present our algorithms, experiment and experiment results. Proposed algorithm allows to solve one of the typical challenges facing autonomous vehicle, particularly finding the optimal plan to safely crossing the intersection. In conclusion we formalized the results and directions for future study.

2 Autonomous vehicle control models

In this study, we consider a group of autonomous vehicles that come to intersection and /or locate at it as a multi-agent robotic system, characterized by the following factors:

- the unpredictable dynamics of the external environment;
- incomplete and contradictory knowledge of robots (agents) about conditions of the external environment and other road users;
- a variety of options for achieving goals, team structures, roles;
- the complexity of providing reliable communications in the distributed multi-agent system.

The goal of developing system is to find a strategy, which allow to generate plan for crossroad intersection for each drone.

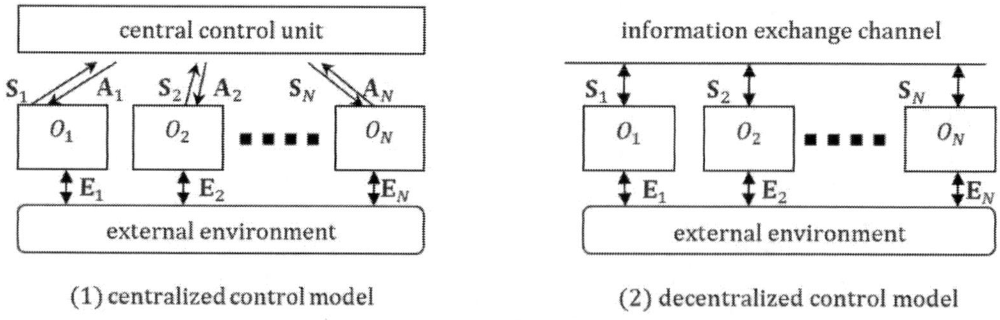

Fig. 1. Swarm robotics control models.

There are two fundamentally different approaches in swarm robotics for control the robots: (1) centralized control model and (2) decentralized control model. They are presented on Fig. 1.

Centralized control model includes central control unit and communication channels with all robots. In [9,10] proposed variety of algorithms for crossing the intersection by autonomous automobiles using a centralized management strategy. They are based on an idea that every intersection should be managed by an autonomous intelligent agent (central control unit). The central control unit or CCU controls each car individually, not a traffic light, which prevents or allows traffic on the entire road. According to one of this algorithms drone O_i comes to an intersection, connect to the CCU, send a message S_i to CCU. Central control unit simulates the situation taking into account other vehicles orders and incorporate O_i into the plan of intersection control due to previously received requests from the environment and other agents.

Significant disadvantages of this approach include: (1) the decision time increases exponentially depending on the number of objects N in a group during usage of centralized group control strategy, and (2) the safety of intersection crossing strongly depends on the reliability of CCU and a communication channel with the agents, that forces to reserve critical communication channel facilities.

Decentralized control strategy bereft this drawback considerably making it an attractive to develop an algorithm for the solution using multi-agent communication and decision-making.

3 The proposed model and its approbation

Traffic management based on swarm intelligence involves the autonomous vehicles route selection which rely on traffic information received from other vehicles. The lack of a single center for decision-making complicates the route selection. It is necessary to define the fundamental principles of interaction and operation of autonomous vehicles to identify some criteria for plan selection and perform experiments in order to estimate the developing model performance.

3.1 Principles of autonomous vehicles interaction

For a complete understanding of the intersection management, we should describe intersection scheme. Schematic representation of investigated road intersection is presented in Fig 2. It contains an intersection of four roads, each may move in one direction only.

Fig. 2. Schematic representation of investigated road intersection.

During traffic from the start of road A to its end, autonomous automobiles, those who choose that route, will cross the intersection with road B. During the distributed intersection management vehicles collaborate at some time point. Let's the road consists of the set of elementary areas $\{p_0 , \dots , p_n\}$. The crossroad is located on the area P_i, $0<i<n$. In this context s represents a maximum speed on the road A It is necessary to provide the interaction with other vehicles from the moment when the vehicle has enough distance for safe braking. Therefore, we need $s+1$ steps to stop. Hence, the full path of the braking is $(s(s+1))/2+1$ elementary areas. In an example that present on the Fig. 2, the car must start the process of interaction with other vehicles at the moment when they located on position

$p_i((s(s+1))/2+1)$. For some simulation simplification, we make a decision that each car starts to communicate with others during that time, despite each car's speed.

Vehicle routing is based on the following basic principles:

1. Turning is performed according to scheme on Fig 3
2. Speed on the turning areas equals 1
3. Speed of moving vehicle on the previous or next time point may differ from the actual speed by more than 1
4. The vehicle tries moving with the maximum speed. At low speeds, it seeks the opportunity to restore it to maximum value
5. Speed more than maximum is unacceptable

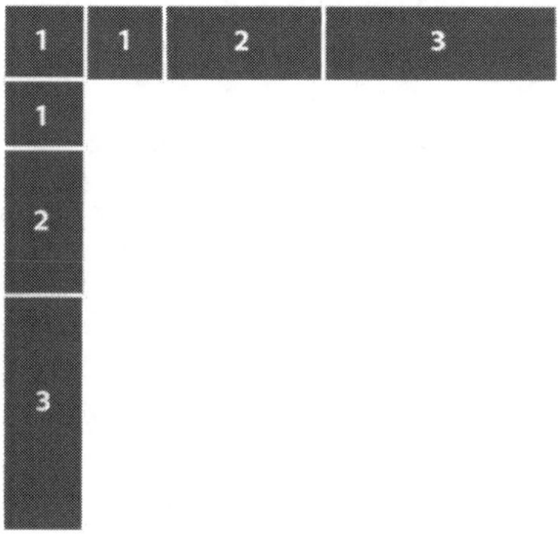

Fig. 3. Schematic representation of investigated road intersection.

Conflict is the point in time when two or more cars locate in the same elementary area. Rerouting proceed according to order of conflict situations occurrence. Each car involved in the conflict must change route using speed reduction. It allows to solve all other conflicts. In a general case, each conflict has two possible crossroad intersection plans. We use a variety of criteria to determine the best possible options.

According to Fig. 3, when the vehicle driving up to the crossroad elementary area after which it will have to change the motion direction, the vehicle must reduce speed to the minimum possible value. Speed reduction is carried out according to the general principles of smooth braking. After the vehicle passed the intersection, it accelerates smoothly to the maximum desired speed.

3.2 Optimization criteria for crossroad intersection plans

Exploring possible criteria of optimal route selection, we determined that the main criteria can be classified into three broad groups, according to the basic parameters of these criteria. In general case the data groups can be represented as follows:

1. Criteria based on collaborated vehicles speed characteristics
2. Criteria based on temporal traffic characteristics
3. Criteria based on the losses in distance due of car's speed reduction

Some concepts, which we will use further, should be clarified in order to consider each of the criteria groups. All vehicle characteristics involved in the process of specifying the routes can be divided into the desirable and real one. Desired characteristics are inherent to moving vehicle in the absence of other cars at the intersection. The actual characteristics are inherent to the vehicles movement after rerouting. Speed, time of location at the crossroad and some spatial characteristics can be both real and desired. Plan of movement should not be modified in the absence of conflict that means the actual characteristics are equal to desired.

It is necessary to enter the main used symbols before the definition of main optimization criteria:

Table 1. Used variables

Variable	Description
v_n^{act}	The average actual speed of the *n*-th car
v_n^{exp}	The average expected speed of the *n*-th car
t_n^{act}	The actual intersection time of the *n* -th car
t_n^{exp}	The expected intersection time of the *n* -th car
d_{tn}^{act}	The actual covered distance of the *n*-th car at the moment *t*
d_{tn}^{exp}	The expected covered distance of the *n*-th car at the moment *t*
N	Number of cars
T_n	Intersection time of *n*-th car
DC_n	Time without maximum speed of *n*-th car

The first criteria group is based on a driving cars speed during collaboration. In this article we use two following criteria from this group:

1. The average actual vehicle speed
2. The average difference between desired and actual speed

The criterion (1) aims to maximize the average speed, the criterion (2) intent to reduce the number of cars decelerations during collaboration. More precisely, the second criterion used for minimizing changes in the moving vehicle speed.

The second criteria group is aimed on optimization of temporal traffic characteristics. These group contain following main criteria:

3. Average actual time vehicles spent at the intersection

The usage of criterion (3) allows us to estimate how much time cars spent at the intersection in absolute numbers.

The third group of criteria is based on the distance losses because of the car did not pass because of forced reduction in speed:

4. Average loss in distance in terms of one unit of time
5. Average loss in distance due to the lower speeds

The criteria in this group are focused on possible reduction of costs from the speed decreasing. The criterion (4) allows us to calculate some costs for each delay, expressed in not traveled distance (the difference between the distance that could be overcome with maximum speed and distance that had been passed in reality), while the criterion (5) aims to minimize each car total losses.

3.3 Performance indicators

It is necessary to define some indicators in order to compare the model performance using each criterion.

Two performance systems are obvious: (1) average vehicle speed and (2) average time vehicle spent on the intersection. These indicators estimate the time needed to each vehicle for intersecting the crossroad.

3.4 Experiment results

3.4.1 A comparison of the classical and proposed model efficiency

Three groups of experiments were conducted on the field, presented in Fig 2. The field is characterized with dimensions 10 at 10. For a proper understanding of the proposed algorithm performance, it was decided to limit the roads to 4 lanes: two vertical (counter and passing) and two horizontal (counter and passing).

Groups of experiments differ in the probability of a vehicle appearance: P = 1.0 (there is at least one new car), P = 0.5 and P = 0.2. The number of appearing cars will be assigned randomly.

The experiments run 1000 times. The duration of each experiment is 1000 steps. Fig. 4 shows the results of the experiment.

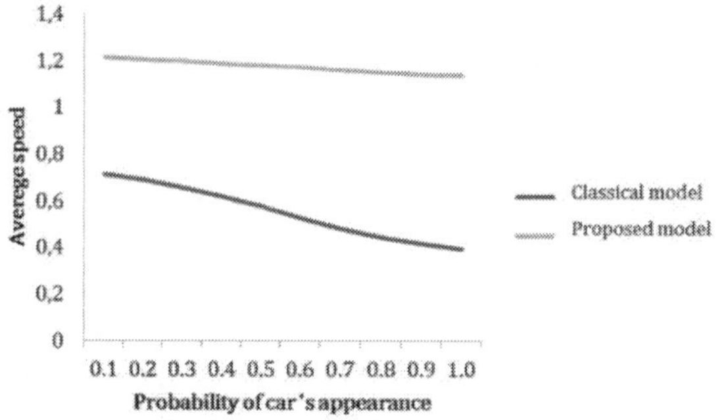

Fig. 4. The dependence of average speed from the probability of car appearance.

Above data represents that the algorithm helps to increase the speed of the crossroad intersection. It is noteworthy that the average traffic speed is decreasing by increasing the flux density in both cases, but this indicator is reduced by 15\% less with the developed algorithm. Furthermore, average speed of autonomous vehicle is three times more, than the same one in classical model.

Average speed is a criterion for the proposed algorithm.

3.4.2 A comparison of the efficiency criteria

In order to compare criteria presented above we use field from Fig. 2. Based on developed model characteristics, experiment results are divided into two broad groups:

1. The probability of the car's appearance on the road less than 0.5;
2. The probability of the car's appearance on the road more than 0.5.

This approach allows imagining the model capabilities under different conditions much better. This group choice is caused by the road capacity: in the first case less than half the road capacity is used and in the second case traffic load tends to reach maximum.

Table 2 presents the results of the model using different criteria for the first case, in Table 3 for the second one.

Table 2. A comparison of proposed model and same one that based on different criteria effectiveness ($Probability < 0,5$).

Criteria	Actual Speed	Expected Speed	Actual Time	Expected Time
1	1,36	1,63	20,61	17,53
2	1,36	1,63	20,59	17,53

3	1,36	1,63	20,38	17,53
4	1,33	1,63	20,90	17,53
5	1,36	1,63	20,53	17,53

Table 3. A comparison of proposed model and same one that based on different criteria effectiveness (*Probability* >= 0,5).

Criteria	Actual Speed	Expected Speed	Actual Time	Expected Time
1	0,89	1,65	38,87	17,43
2	0,90	1,65	38,08	17,39
3	0,68	1,65	40,38	17,44
4	0,81	1,65	41,95	17,44
5	0,68	1,65	41,01	17,42

As we can see from Table 2 and Table 3 different criteria should be used for different traffic options. It is much better to use criteria based on temporal road characteristics for cases with low congestion (it allows to reduce the actual time spent on the intersection). However, in case of a high workload, this criterion work slightly worse than any criterion, based on speed characteristics.

4 Conclusion

In this paper, we introduce a model for multi-agent car traffic planning, several optimization criteria for intersection plan, experiment performance in order to determine the efficiency of the proposed model with different criteria. The finding of the conducted experiments present, that the proposed model for intersection traffic management able to regulate the traffic more efficiently, due to increased autonomous vehicles average speed.

The results presented here may facilitate improvements in the further research taking into account the previously obtained results and new theoretical developments, regarding reduce of traffic congestion. Besides, we plan to evaluate the information security of the proposed model, analyse its resistance to destructive influences and develop protection methods from possible damage caused by the implementation of different threats.

References

1. Milanés V. et al. *Clavileño. Evolution of an autonomous car.* 13th Int. IEEE Conf. on ITSC, 1129-1134 (2010)
2. Varaiya P. *Smart cars on smart roads: problems of control.* IEEE Trans. on Autom. Cont. **38**, 2 (1993)
3. Bazzan A.L.C. *A Distributed Approach for Coordination of Traffic Signal Agents.* Autonomous Agents and Multi-Agent Systems. **10**, 1 (2005)
4. Beeson P. etc. *Multi-agent Interactions in Urban Driving.* J.of Phys.. **2**, 1 (2008)
5. Hallé S., Chaib-draa B. *A collaborative driving system based on multiagent modelling and simulations.* Transp. Res. Part C: Emerging Technologies. **13**, 4 (2005)
6. Carlino D., Boyles S. D., Stone P. *Auction-based autonomous intersection management.*.16th Int.IEEE Conf.on ITSC, 529-534 (2013)

7. Wuthishuwong C., Traechtler A.: *Vehicle to infrastructure based safe trajectory planning for Autonomous Intersection Management.* 13th Int. Conf. on ITST, 175-180 (2013)
8. Vahidi A., Eskandarian A. *Research advances in intelligent collision avoidance and adaptive cruise control.* IEEE Trans.on Intel. Transp. Syst. **4**, 3 (2003)
9. Ho C., Reed N., Spence C. *Multisensory in-car warning signals for collision avoidance*. The Journal of the Human Factors and Ergonomics Society. **49**, 6 (2007)
10. Au T., Zhang S., Stone P. *Autonomous Intersection Management for Semi-Autonomous Vehicles.* Handbook of Transportation. 88-104 (2015)
11. Dresner K., Stone P. *A multiagent approach to autonomous intersection management*. Journal of artificial intelligence research. 591-656 (2008)
12. Wu J., Abbas-Turki A., El Moudni A. *Cooperative driving: an ant colony system for autonomous intersection management.* Appl. Int. **37**, 2 (2012)
13. Zohdy I. H., Kamalanathsharma R. K., Rakha H. *Intersection management for autonomous vehicles using icacc*. 15th Int. IEEE Conf. on ITS, 1109-1114 (2012)

ITM Web of Conferences **8**, 01008 (2016) DOI: 10.1051/itmconf/20160801008
ICBDA 2016

Non-convex polygons clustering algorithm

Alexey Kruglikov[1,*], and *Mikhail* Vasilenko[1]

[1]Ural Federal University, Yekaterinburg, Russia

Abstract. A clustering algorithm is proposed, to be used as a preliminary step in motion planning. It is tightly coupled to the applied problem statement, i.e. uses parameters meaningful only with respect to it. Use of geometrical properties for polygons clustering allows for a better calculation time as opposed to general-purpose algorithms. A special form of map optimized for quick motion planning is constructed as a result.

1 Introduction

A variety of real-world applications require using random maps of complex structure; similar problems arise in computational dynamics [1], blood flow dynamical simulation [2], and motion planning for limited maneuverability objects [3].

Specific kinds of maritime motion planning problems exist where it is important to consider all the obstacles charted on the map. In case of a major archipelago and reasonable level of detail this could mean dealing with thousands of islands described with up to tens of thousands points each, which is costly in terms of computational resources. A motion planning algorithm currently developed in Ural Federal University is trying to reduce costs by working on a pre-clustered map. This paper is concerned with an algorithm of preliminary clustering.

Approach used is similar to hierarchical clustering [4], its specific features are as follows:

- hierarchy has a fixed number of levels;
- different clustering procedures are used for different levels;
- different properties are inherent to clusters of different levels.

2 Problem and terms

Consider a map with charted obstacles, which may be represented as a two-dimensional Cartesian coordinate system and a set of polygons with coordinates measured in it. It is assumed that polygons are identified by unique names or indexes, have no self-intersections, and do not intersect pairwise. Also a positive constant value R_{max} is defined, meaning minimal safe distance from an obstacle the vehicle in question should not violate.

Such obstacles clusters must be found that their convex geometric borders had at least $2 R_{max}$ distance pairwise, i.e. allowed safe movement between them.

[*]a.s.kruglikov@urfu.ru

It is convenient to use the following notations:

- *Frame* is a minimal rectangle aligned along coordinate axes and containing a nonempty set of polygons.
- *Container* is a set of polygons with one member marked as main, used as a low-level polygon cluster.
- *Container family* is a nonempty set of containers, mid-level polygon cluster.
- *Families group* is a nonempty set of families, highest-level polygon cluster.
- *Rough hull* is a convex hull of a set of frames, used as a polygon cluster geometrical border.

3 Algorithm

Clustering is done in a "bottom-up" fashion in four steps:

- frames are calculated for the polygons;
- polygons are clustered into containers;
- containers are clustered into families;
- families are clustered into groups.

It is noteworthy that the first two steps can benefit from parallel implementation. They are also discussed in greater detail since are most important and time-consuming.

Frame calculation and container clustering. A frame for a polygon is calculated by brute force; it represents a polygon in the rest of clustering process. In essence, two issues are addressed: all the polygons of original data widely varying in their properties are given unified representation, and also data dimension is reduced. What is lost in precision is compensated for by lower calculation time given typically long and complex polygon boundaries.

Definition. A *container*, notation *C*, is a set of polygons with one member marked as main such that all polygons' frames are included as geometrical shapes into main polygon frame; the latter is also the frame of the container itself.

A container might not include the frame of another container.

In the following P_i is used to denote a polygon with index *i*, while its frame is denoted as F_i; P_0 denotes main element, and $F(C)$ is containers frame.

$$C = \{ P_i \mid \forall i > 0 : F_i \subset F_0 \}$$

$$F(C) = F_0$$

$$C_1 \neq C_2 \rightarrow F(C_1) \not\subset F(C_2) \wedge F(C_2) \not\subset F(C_1) \tag{1}$$

Figure 1 shows polygons and corresponding containers, the latter depicted by their frames. It is convenient to identify a container by its main member name.

Container clustering algorithm operates a dynamic list *CL* of currently found containers. Any freshly constructed frame representing polygon *P* is checked for nesting into each current container. There could only be three cases:

- A frame is included into at least one container frame. Then *P* becomes member to each container it fits into.
- A frame fits into no current container; *P* becomes a new one-element container in *CL*.
- A frame includes a frame of at least one current container. A new container with *P* as main member is put into *CL*, while included containers are removed, and all their members are transferred to the new container.

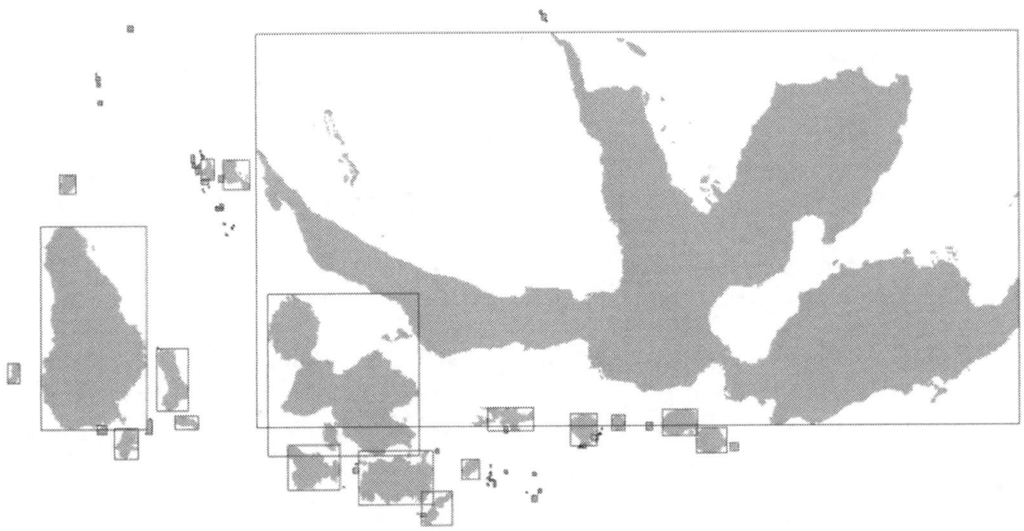

Fig. 1. Containers.

Proposition 1. Container clustering algorithm guarantees that (1) holds.
Proof. Assume $\exists C_1 \neq C_2 : F(C_1) \subseteq F(C_2)$.

If C_1 was constructed later than C_2, then at the moment of its main member *P* frame analysis C_2 was in the current containers list. Since

$$F(P) = F(C_1) \subseteq F(C_2),$$

P should have been included into C_2 and any other container it fitted into. Therefore, to have *P* as its main element C_1 should have already existed by the time it was constructed, which is impossible.

If C_2 was constructed later than C_1, then at the moment its main element *P* frame was analyzed C_1 was in the current container list. Since

$$F(C_1) \subseteq F(C_2) = F(P),$$

C_1 should have been removed from the list at that moment. But C_1 exists, so it must have been added later, which is impossible as was already shown.

qed

It is worth noting that calculation of frame nesting typically also yields information on frames intersection which is useful for the next step and could be stored. For that a list for intersecting containers registration is attached to each container, all the containers intersecting the frame are stored in a list *L*, and the following logic is used after the frame is checked for nesting:

- If a container includes a frame, then it intersects frames of all containers in *L*.
- If *P* becomes a new one-element container, it intersects all containers in *L*.
- If a frame includes one or more containers, it intersects frames of all containers in *L* plus all containers the nested ones did intersect, and minus containers included.

At the end of clustering procedure all the containers in *CL* are checked for their lists of intersections, and the latter are merged into an undirected graph *G* of intersections. For the later discussion it is important that all the containers intersections are thus found.

Proposition 2. If container clustering algorithm stores intersection information, all container intersections are found.

Proof. Assume $\exists C_1, C_2 : F(C_1) \cap F(C_2) \neq \varnothing$, but G does not contain rib (C_1, C_2).

If C_1 was constructed later, then at the moment of its main element P frame analysis C_2 was in a list of current containers. Then a list L of frame-intersecting containers for P did have C_2 in it. The only chance to miss C_2 in the list of C_1 is to drop it since C_2 was included into C_1, which is not true.

If C_2 was constructed later, the same logic shows C_2 must have C_1 in its list.

Either way graph G obtains rib (C_1, C_2), which contradicts assumption.

qed

Complexity and parallelism. The best case for the algorithm is obviously when the first frame contains all the rest, and it is enough to do one check for each frame at a cost of $O(N)$ operations where N is the number of polygons. The worst case is the opposite, when all the frames but the last are independent though maybe intersecting, while the last is including all of them. At least N^2 operations are needed then.

That said, it is obvious that in a sequential implementation algorithm would benefit from preliminary sorting of frames, and it would be natural to sort frames by their area.

Parallel implementation should consider the following: frame calculation can be much more time-consuming than a step of clustering, so it is possible to link two procedures in a pipeline fashion. Container clustering itself does intersection checking of a frame independently, so it could be easily implemented parallel, but editing the CL list prevents it from checking two different frames simultaneously. Also, since short-length polygons will usually get their frames calculated faster, clustering will often start with smaller polygons, which is undesirable. With respect to that a parallel implementation could be as follows.

Frames calculation is done with as much parallelism as possible. Container clustering procedure operates a buffer of incoming frames and starts only when a buffer is full. It then copies buffer contents, clears buffer, sorts copied frames by their area and runs sequentially, maybe using parallelism when checking frame nesting/intersection with different members of CL list. While that is done, a buffer is getting new frames for the next round of container clustering.

Family clustering. After all polygons are sorted into containers further clustering is done based on container frames intersection.

Definition. *Container family*, notation CF, is a nonempty set of containers such that for each two different members there exists a sequence of frame-intersecting members of the same family connecting them.

Containers from different families might not have intersecting frames.

$$CF = \{C_i\}$$

$$\forall C_i, C_j \in CF \; \exists C_{k_0}, \ldots, C_{k_n} \in CF : C_{k_0} = C_i, C_{k_n} = C_j, F\left(C_{k_l}\right) \cap F\left(C_{k_{l+1}}\right) \neq \varnothing$$

$$CF_1 \neq CF_2 \rightarrow \forall C_1 \in CF_1, C_2 \in CF_2 \; F(C_1) \cap F(C_2) = \varnothing$$

If the previous step did use information on frames intersection, which is preferable, then graph G of intersections is already constructed, and a family is a simply connected component in it. As was shown, all container intersections are found by the previous step, which guarantees correct families construction.

Otherwise graph G is to be calculated in a separate step of $O(N^2)$ complexity where N is number of containers. Family clustering algorithm is a simplified form of single-link clustering [5].

Figure 2 shows containers from Figure 1 clustered into families depicted by red borders.

 DOI: 10.1051/itmconf/20160801008

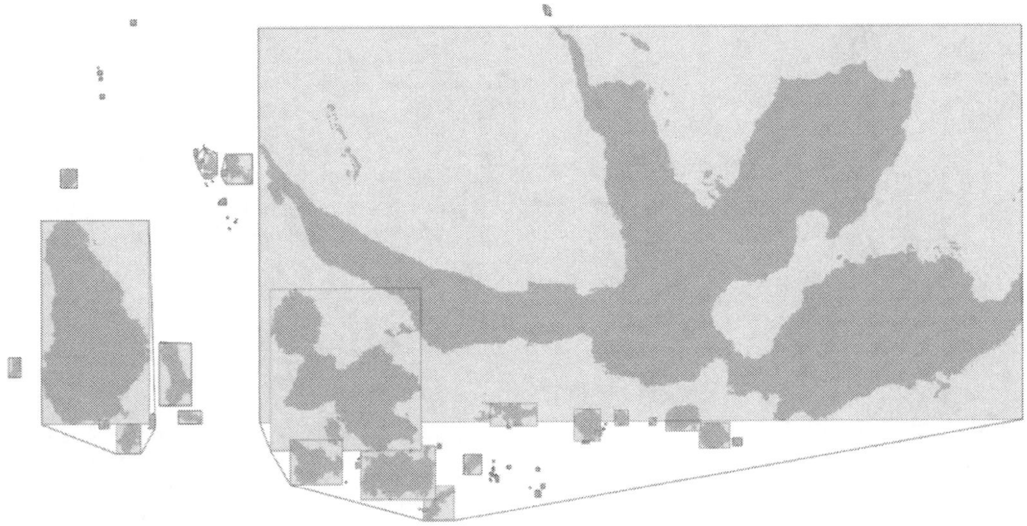

Fig. 2. Container families.

Groups clustering. To cluster families into groups each of the former is assigned a rough hull; it is worth noting that rough hulls of different families might be intersecting or even included as geometrical shapes. Different groups should have their rough hulls no closer than 2 R_{max}; intersection or close distance between them invoke merging. Figure 3 shows several families groups depicted by red borders; families from Figure 2 can be seen in the upper right corner.

Used algorithm is also a modification of single-link clustering, but is done in two steps, and distance is not derived from distances between families but rather recalculated as a distance between groups' rough hulls. First, groups are formed of families with intersecting or nested rough hulls. This step is finished when all the groups have non-intersecting rough hulls. The second step uses R_{max} and merges groups with distances lower than twice that value. Resulting groups have their rough hulls no closer than 2 R_{max} to each other, which is the solution for the stated problem.

Second step is distinguished for the following reason: all the steps before it are only using polygons coordinates and thus produce natural clustering, which could be saved and reused with different values assigned to R_{max}.

Land clusters hierarchy. As a result a four-level land clusters hierarchy is formed with levels of:

- polygons and their respective frames;
- containers and their respective frames;
- families and their respective rough hulls;
- family groups and their respective rough hulls.

 DOI: 10.1051/itmconf/20160801008

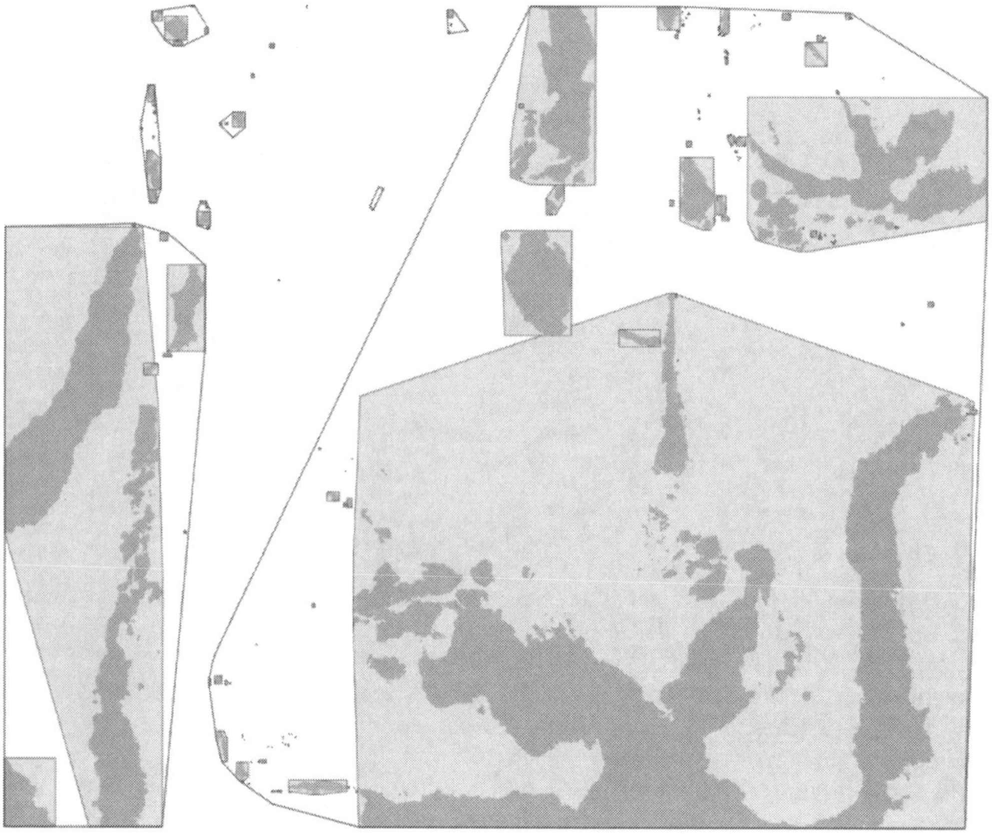

Fig. 3. Families groups.

4 Conclusion

Described algorithm is implemented in C++ and is used as part of route planning implementation. It was tested on real-world data and has demonstrated results presented by figures in this paper. The case depicted had 1031 polygons which were clustered into 310 containers, 201 families and 12 families groups.

It must be noted that a cluster does not imply there is no free movement between its member islands. Figure 3 allows to discern wide passages inside the largest families group. This is a serious drawback from route planning point of view, and it is addressed by another algorithm which further refines the specialized map representation, but is not discussed in this paper.

References

1. V.P. Ilyin, South Ural State University Bulletin **35** 29-40 (2011)
2. T.K. Dobroserdova et al., *IFMBE Proceedings* **6** 403-406 (2015)
3. S.V. Kruglikov, A.S. Kruglikov, Applied Mechanics and Materials. **494-495** 1110-1113 (2014)
4. A. Jain, M. Murty, P. Flynn, ACM Computing Surveys. **31** (1999)
5. P.H. Sneath, R.P. Sokal, *Numerical taxonomy. The principles and practice of numerical classification.* (Freeman, London, UK, 1973).

ITM Web of Conferences **8**, 01009 (2016) DOI: 10.1051/itmconf/20160801009
ICBDA 2016

Applying of the NVIDIA CUDA to the video processing in the task of the roundwood volume estimation

Artem Kruglov[1,*], *Andrey* Chiryshev[1], and *Evgeniya* Shishko[1]

[1] Ural Federal University, 32 Mira street, Yekaterinburg, Russian Federation

Abstract. The paper is devoted to the parallel computing. The algorithm for roundwood volume estimation had insufficient performance so it was decided to port its bottleneck part on the GPU. The analysis of various GPGPU techniques was observed and the NVIDIA CUDA technology was chosen for implementation. The results of the research have shown the high potential of the GPU implementation in the improvement performance of the computation. The speedup of the algorithm for the roundwood volume estimation is more than 300% after porting on GPU with implementation of the CUDA technology. This helps to apply the machine vision algorithm in real-time system.

1 Introduction

Nowadays the GPGPU (General Purpose Computing on Graphic Processing Units) technology has come into widespread acceptance [1]. This programming technique is embedded in the data-flow computing concept. Data-flow computing is the paradigm of parallel computing that interpret data to be processed as a thread which elements could be processed independently hence parallel [2].
Hardware-software architecture CUDA (Compute Unified Device Architecture) developed by the NVIDIA is the implementation of the GPGPU technology. CUDA provides high-level language (C and C++) programming to solve the complex computational problem in a less time due to the multi-core processing power of the GPU [3].

2 The analysis of the parallelization possibility

The R&D project "Hardware-software system for assessment of cubic capacity and type of wood" (grant number 14418/8880 of the FASIE fund) in a part of the software development has resulted in the set of the algorithms for the solving the problem of the roundwood volume measurement via video analysis. All computations referred to the image processing were optimized to running on CPU. The flow diagram of the algorithm is given in the Figure 1.

* Corresponding author: avkruglov@yandex.ru

The sequential implementation gives an insufficient performance of the algorithm thatprevents its implementation in the real-time data processing [4]. The speedupof the algorithm is possible via its adaption to the parallel architecture.

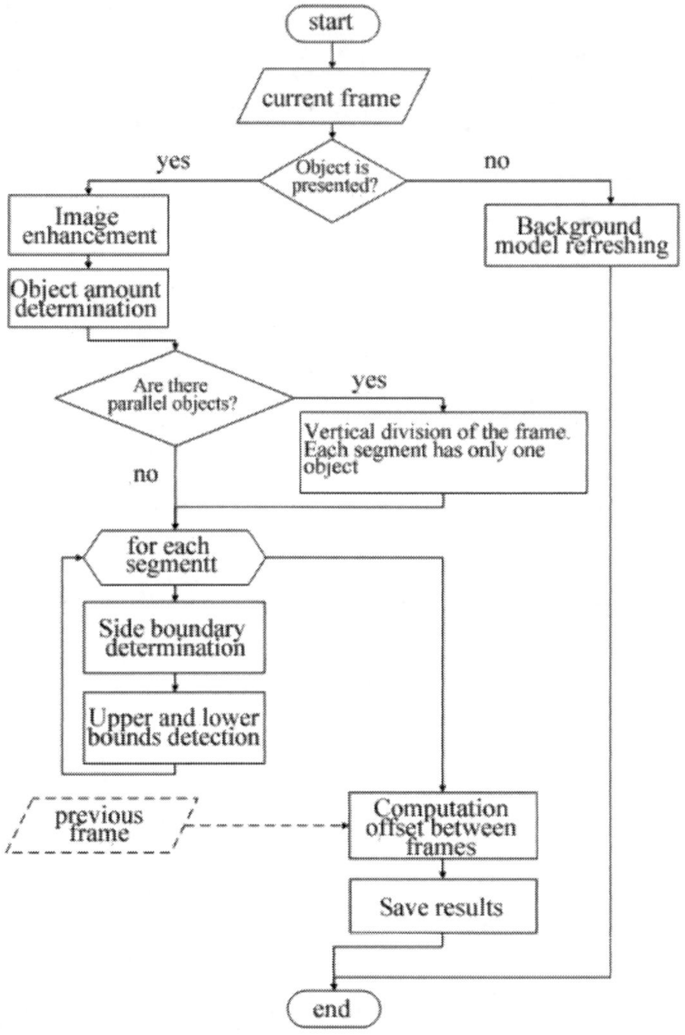

Fig. 1. Flow diagram of the roundwood volume estimation algorithm.

The first step of the algorithm porting on the GPU is its profiling and determination of the time-consuming code areas which need the parallelizing [5]. The complete porting of the algorithm is impossible due to the fact that the GPU has access neither to the memory nor to the input-output devices of the PC inasmuch as it is an auxiliary tool for computing [6]. The computational experiment was carried out to determine the bottleneck of the algorithm. For that purpose a number of the images showing the various cases in the process of the roundwood volume estimation were sampled (Table 1).

Table 1. Set of the images.

№	1	2
Image		
Description	No objects	Appearance of the object
№	3	4
Image		
Description	Tracking of the object	End of the object
№	5	6
Image		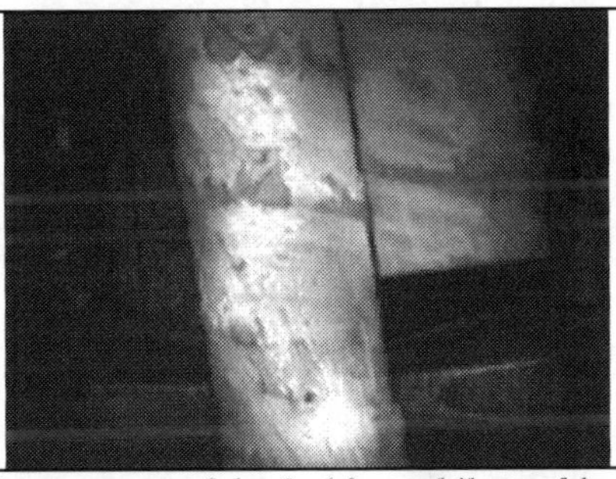
Description	End of the 1 object and top of the 2 object	Appearance of the 2 object while tracking the 1 object
№	7	
Image	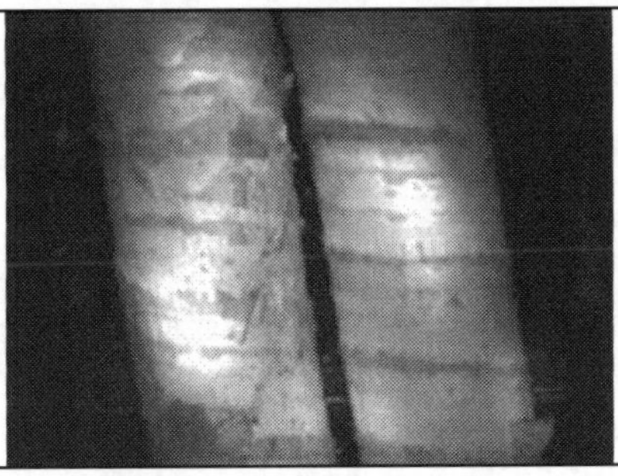	
Description	Tracking of two objects	

The algorithm itself was divided into three basic parts:
- image enhancement,
- background model refreshing,
- detection.

The CPU processing time for each part of the algorithm was measured. Results of the computational experiment are given in the Table 2.

Table 2. Results of the computational experiment.

Image	Processing time, ms			
	Image enhancement	Background model refreshing	Object detection	Total
1	0	2,1	0	2,1
2	31,4	0	10,6	42,0
3	32,0	0	11,5	43,5
4	31,9	0	12,0	43,9
5	32,1	0	13,0	45,1
6	31,9	0	13,6	45,5
7	32,2	0	13,4	45,6

The experiment showed that the bottleneck of the algorithm is image enhancement. This operation consumes about 70% of the time of the frame sequence processing. The image enhancement consists of the combination of the basic morphology operators which are the erosion and dilatation. The consequent execution of these methods of the non-linear signal processing is an extremely effective approach to noise reduction within the developed algorithm [7, 8, 9].

The mentioned morphology operators are referred to the group of the local transformation and implemented in sliding mode by successive displacement of the scanning area which includes an odd number of image samplings. All pixels occurring in the scanning area are processed by the specific scenario [10]. The result of the processing is a output image pixel referred to the center of the scanning area. The final value of the pixel is computed as a minimum value among all pixels in the area for the erosion and a maximum value for the dilatation [11]. Since each pixel is processed by the same consequence of the operation (minimum and maximum search), the algorithm could be effectively implemented on the GPU [3, 12].

3 The implementation of the algorithm on GPU

The structure of the image enhancement algorithm using CUDA consists of the following steps:

1. Selecting of the active GPU;
2. Allocating the data store for an image in the global memory;
3. Loading input image into the global memory;
4. Loading coefficients of the filter window into the constant memory;
5. Forming the structure of the computational grid;
6. Launching the kernel functions executing the image filtration;
7. Copying the output image from the GPU memory to the internal memory;
8. Deallocating.

 DOI: 10.1051/itmconf/20160801009

The code is written on CUDA C and consists of the sections which executed on both the CPU and GPU [13]. The host-code with a description is listed below.

```
#define BLOCK_DIM 16
__constant__ int c_mask[25];
// Host-function
void FilterGPU (byte *inbuf, byte *outbuf, int height,
int width, int apert, int *mask)
{
// Device initialization
cudaSetDevice(0);
// Memory allocating
byte *buf;
cudaMalloc ((void **)&buf, sizeof(byte)*width*height);
// Loading image into the device
cudaMemcpy (buf,inbuf, sizeof(byte)*width*height,
cudaMemcpyHostToDevice);
// Loading coefficients of the filter window into the
constant memory
cudaMemcpyToSymbol («c_mask», mask,
sizeof(int)*apert*apert);
// Computational grid forming
dim3 blocks = dim3(width/BLOCK_DIM+1,
height/BLOCK_DIM+1);
dim3 threads = dim3(BLOCK_DIM, BLOCK_DIM);
// Kernel launch
kernel <<<blocks, threads>>> (buf, height, width, apert);
cudaThreadSynchronize();
// Uploading output image to the PC memory
cudaMemcpy (outbuf, buf, sizeof(byte)*width*height,
cudaMemcpyDeviceToHost);
// Device deallocating
cudaFree(buf);
}
```

4 Comparison of the approaches

The parallel implementation of the image enhancement was implemented to optimize the algorithm of the roundwood volume estimation. The computational experiment was carried out to compare the performance of the parallel implementation on GPU against the sequential implementation on CPU and OpenMP multithreading technology. The three versions of the algorithm were tested on the set of the images. The computational experiment has been carried out on the IBM PC with the following characteristics:

- 8-core CPU Intel Core i7 920 2.79 GHz;
- GPU NVIDIA GeForce GTS 450 (192 CUDA kernels);
- 64x Windows 7 OS.

Compilation of the parallel and sequential versions was implemented in Microsoft Visual Studio 2013, plugin NSight Visual Studio Edition v3.2 and NVIDIA CUDA Toolkit v5.5 were used for parallel implementation. Results of the experiment are presented in the Table 3.

Table 3. Results of the computational experiment.

Image	Average processing time, ms			Speedup (serial)	Speedup (OpenMP)
	Serial	OpenMP	CUDA		
1	2,1	2,1	2,1	1	1
2	42,0	19,9	12,2	3,44	1,63
3	43,5	21,0	12,8	3,4	1,64
4	43,9	21,8	13,9	3,16	1,57
5	45,1	22,9	14,5	3,11	1,57
6	45,5	22,8	15,2	2,99	1,5
7	45,6	22,8	15,4	2,96	1,48
Average (with image enhancement)				3,17	1,56

As can be seen from the Table 3, the average frame processing speedup is more than 300%. Although the average data transfer time to/from GPU is 0,2 ms, the achieved speedup value clearly demonstrates the efficiency of computing on the GPU.

5 Conclusion

The following problems were solved while porting the existent sequential algorithm on the GPU:

- The existing algorithm for roundwood volume estimation was analyzed for the most effective paralleling on GPU;
- The parallel implementation of the algorithm based on the CUDA technology was offered;
- The performance of the algorithm is improved in three times due to the parallelization. This allows to apply the algorithm for the roundwood volume estimation in the real-time systems.

Thus the results of the research have shown the high potential of the GPU implementation in the improvement performance of the computation. The speedup of the ported algorithm provides the resources for additional functionality in the developed hardware-software system of the roundwood estimation. It was decided to use two color digital video cameras which will enable to analyze the major part of the log surface hence support an external estimation of the timber quality.

References

1. D. Kornev, A. Tarhanov, Image processing by the GPU via CUDA technology. In: Proceedings of the 40th Regional Youth Conference, series "Problems of the theoretic and applied mathematics". pp. 406-410 (2009)
2. A. Boreskov, A. Harlanov, Fundamentals of CUDA technology, DMK Press (2010)
3. Nvidia CUDA C programming guide (2015)
4. A.V. Boreskov et al., Parallel computing on GPU. CUDA architectural and programming model. In: Moscow Univ. Proceedings, series "Supercomputer Educations", p. 336 (2012).
5. L. Dorosinsky, V. Kruglov, N. Papylovskaya, A. Chiryshev, CUDA technology in digital image processing tasks. The success of modern science, vol. 10,pp. 88-98(2011)
6. V. Kruglov, N. Papylovskaya, A. Chiryshev, Benefits of sharing CPU and CUDA-device, Fundamental research, vol. 8 № 2,pp. 296-304 (2014)

7. A. Kruglov, V. Kruglov, A. Chiryshev, U. Chiryshev, Implementation of the resource-intensive machine vision algorithms in real-time systems. Fundamental research, vol. 10 № 12,pp. 2612-2619 (2013)
8. R. Tomakova, Hard-segmented image processing method using multi-layer morphological operators. In: Proceedings of the Southwestern State Univ, vol. 2 pp. 158-164 (2012)
9. V. Chernoysov, A. Savchenko, Morphological moving object detection algorithm on noisy video. International scientific-technical conference Information systems and technologies (2014)
10. F. Kornilov, Search structural imaging differences: Algorithms and methods. Machine Learning and Data Analysis, vol. 1 № 7, pp. 902-919 (2014)
11. T. Volosatova, A. Marchenkov, N. Chichvarin, Research and development of the combined method of detection and identification of moving objects. Information Technology, vol. 12, pp. 24-31 (2013)
12. R. Fernando, D. Kirk, GPU gems: Programming techniques, tips and tricks for real-time graphics (2015).
13. T. R. Halfhill, Parallel processing with CUDA (2008).

One Approach to intellectual image analysis

Nikolai Bellustin[1], *Konstantin* Moiseev[2], *Olga* Shemagina[3], *Sergey* Starkov[2*] and *Aleksandr* Telnykh[3]

[1]Radiophisical Research Institute, Nizhny Novgorod, Russia
[2]National Research Nuclear University MEPhI, Obninsk, Russia
[3]Institute of Applied Physics, Russian Academy of Sciences, Nizhny Novgorod, Russia

Abstract. This study investigated the method of semantic image analysis by using a set of neuron-like detectors of foreground objects. This method is intended to find different types of foreground objects and to determine properties of these objects. As a result of semantic analysis the semantic descriptor of the image is created. The descriptor is a set of foreground objects of the image and a set of properties for each object. The distance between images is defined as distance between their semantic descriptors. Using the concept of distance between images, "semantically similarity" between images or videos is defined.

1 Statement of the problem

Fast development of computers, Internet and robotics technologies last years leads to significant increase of interest in image understanding systems. Here we discuss the systems of understanding images which are presented by the array of numbers and contain the description of the scene in "non-visual" form. The type of the scene description depends on the specific task. In some cases, it is desirable to have the description as an indication of the presence or absence of the specified object in the scene, or the appearance of an unexpected object, for example, this approach is useful for use in security systems. Or perhaps it is necessary to track the movement and direction of some object, this task can be used in surveillance systems. In more complex cases, such a system could create a general description of the scene, which contains the main elements of the scene and the list of objects in it. Modern researches focus on the development of such programmable systems that could process a wide class of images arising in a wide variety of applications, including compression, storage and video analysis. There are already created systems, which perform relatively simple images description for limited class of images [1-2].

The image analysis process is carried out in several stages. In the first phase in the observed image the simplest features are extracted, the features may be natural in the sense that they are established by visual analysis of the image, while other artificial features are obtained as a result of its special processing or measurements. Natural features include such features as brightness of the image elements, the coordinates of contour points, form objects, etc. To highlight these characteristics in the different methods of contour extraction

* Corresponding author: sergeystarkov56@mail.ru

are used, making two level images (binarization), or N-level images [1-2]. The artificial features are histograms of brightness distribution, spectra of spatial frequencies, the results of the processing of Haar cascades [3]. Then this feature set goes to the block symbolic representation, which forms the characters of the features. For example, contour points are grouped into line segments or closed curves, elements with the same brightness etc. These objects description already has semantic representation.

A coherent semantic description of the object is formed by using these semantic characteristics, and it allows making the categorization and identification of detected objects. The information obtained is stored in a general database and can be used for further search. The comparison of proximity between the images is already made on the basis of these semantic descriptions.

But this approach gives a number of issues making the procedure very difficult and sometimes essentially impossible. There are changes in brightness, scale, angle of view and the registered image angle. Serious limitations also appear in case of registered movement of the camera relative to the scene objects. In this case, the so-called semantic gap – the absence of adequate matching between the low-level descriptive features of the graphical object (color, brightness, relative positions and sizes of fragments, etc.) and its semantic description. Schematically this is presented in Figure 1. [2012 Hewlett-Packard Development Company, L. P.].

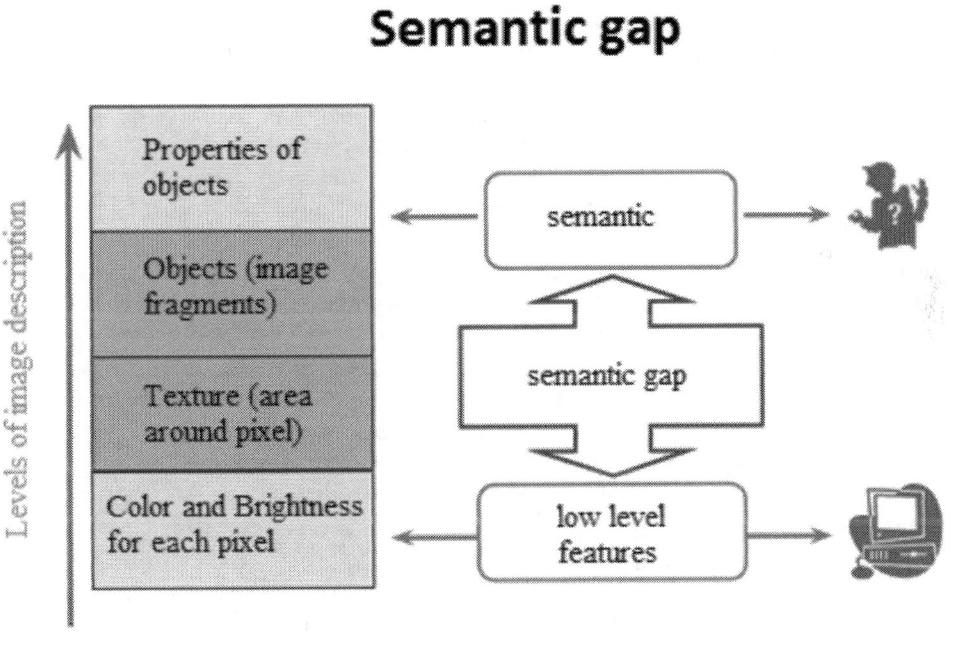

Fig. 1. The semantic gap the analysis of the graphic images.

2 Key idea

In this paper we consider one possible approach to constructing semantic descriptions of registered scenes image, for its subsequent use for effective analysis of graphic images and video scenes.

2.1 Video data signatures

The basic idea is to use the totality of the intellectual video detection, which allows to carry out detection and identification of particular classes of objects at the stage of primary video recording. An example of such a video detector, for instance, may be a video face detector, widely used currently in a various applications: smartphones, authentication system, etc. If we assume that we have setup VMD under a unique object (a person, object, figure, angle, shape/s, action, moving, etc.), the descriptors of individual objects, their relative positions would accurately reflect the specific scene.

Often, to help you find the desired graphic information in large databases of images and videos, formal external description of the data, called metadata are used. Signatures of images and videos in a sense can also be considered as metadata, as are formal appearance, relative to the source image information description. Video data signatures, in the form of metadata, depend only on the algorithm for generating signatures and on the data.

In this work, we propose to overcome the semantic gap between mathematical and semantic description of video data using the technique of "semantic analysis of video information".

In the application to static images the semantic analysis consists of the designation of certain areas or the whole mage by units of a natural language, and in the application to video – dynamic scenes marking by units of natural language.

A tool that is able to automatically designate a certain area of the image is a detector of objects of the specified type and tracker, which provides support for found objects from frame to frame [3, 4]. The nature of the detector can be different - neural network, cascade connection, based on the color or the contour analysis, texture analysis and so on. The same applies to the nature of the tracker. Important property of the detector is the space localization of object in the image with which it is associated, and for the tracker the main property is the localization of the object in time. The detector indicates the presence of something described by the noun with which it is associated.

Significant expansion of functionality of the proposed system gives us possibilities for analysis of localized detector regions property.

The properties of image area found by the detector is represented by the detector attributes [5], which describes some of the field characteristics by an adjective. Thus, we have a relationship between the noun, its properties, and the detector, the detector attributes and the region on the image. This relationship is the basis of semantic analysis of the static image. And localization of the object found in time using a tracker can be described by a verb of natural language.

The Bank of various detectors, there are a few detectors that analyze the image at the same time, correspond to the controlled vocabulary system for semantic image analysis. The volume of the dictionary says about possibilities of semantic analysis of images. For larger size dictionary semantic analysis will be more pure and complete.

2.2. The primary result

The primary result of the semantic analysis of image is the following table:

Table 1. Semantic signature of image.

ID	Object type	Object size	Object angle	Object location	Attribute 1	…	Attribute N
	Object identifier. Corresponds to type of detector (face, pedestrian, auto, etc.)	Object size feature	Object angle feature	In center, in border, left, right, up, down, et cetera	Object attribute. Takes values (-2,-1,0,1)	.	Object attribute. Takes values (-2,-1,0,1)

The Table 1 is named as semantic signature of image.

On figure 2 an example of semantic signature forming is shown.

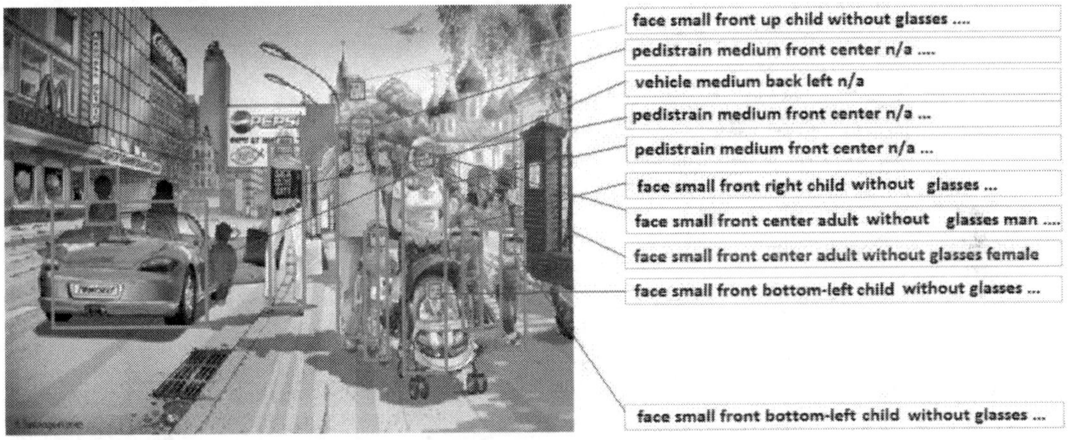

Fig. 2. The formation of semantic signatures image using a Bank of videodetection objects and attributes detectors.

2.2.1 Distance between the images

As shown above, to describe the image so-called "semantic signatures" are used, which can be represented in the form of a table. The semantic description of the image is a set $V=\{\vec{v}_1..\vec{v}_n\}$, which every element $\vec{v}_i=\{[\![x_1]\!]^i..[\![x_k]\!]^i\}, i=(1,n)$ describes the properties of a specific fragment of an image. The elements of these vectors form a set for description of the properties of the fragment obtained using available detectors and object detectors attributes. To build the system, we need to introduce the definition of distance between semantic descriptions of images, the example is presented in Figure 2. To solve the problem, we introduce the following definitions:

Recoding. This encoding is used to represent each element of the vector $\vec{v} = \{x\_1..x\_k\}$, in the form of a number.

The **distance** between two vectors $\vec{v} = \{x\_1..x\_k\}$ that describes some fragment of an image.

The **distance** between the sets $V = \{\vec{v}\_1..\vec{v}\_n\}$ that describes the entire image and is its semantic description.

2.2.2 Decoding and comparison of codes

This encoding is used to represent each element of the vector $\vec{v} = \{x\_1..x\_k\}$ in the form of a code number corresponding to a particular property of the found object. Consider the elements of a vector in more detail. They are in general, correspond to the columns of Table 1. In particular:

- Object type
- Object size
- Object location
- Object angle
- Object attributes

The recoding of an object type is presented in Table 2.

Table 2. The recoding of an object type.

Detector name	Object name	Code
Face detector	People face	1
Pedestrian detector	People pedestrian	2
Car detector	Car	3

The recoding of an object scale is presented in Table 3.

Table 3. The recoding of an object scale.

Object scale	Square criterion	Code
Very large	>50%	1
Large	>20% <50%	2
Medium	>5% <20%	3
Little	<5%	4

The recoding of an object location is presented in Table 4.

Table 4. The recoding of an object location.

Object location	Code
In the center	1
In the left	2
In the right	3
At the top	4
At the bottom	5
Top-left	6
Top-right	7
bottom-right	8
bottom-left	9

The recoding of an object angle is presented in Table 5.

Table 5. The recoding of an object angle.

Object angle	Code
Straight	1
Straight-left	2
Straight-right	3
Left	4
Right	5
Behind	6
Behind-left	7
Behind-right	8

The recoding of an attribute is presented in Table 6.

Table 6. The recoding of an attribute.

Attribute disponibility	Code
It is impossible to determine attribute	-2
Attribute is absent	-1
Attribute is present	1
Attribute is not determined	0

For comparison the corresponding codes x_i describe the fragment of an image use the binary function (1).

$$h_i^{km} = \begin{cases} 1, x_i^k \neq x_i^m \\ 0, x_i^k = x_i^{m}, \end{cases} \quad (1)$$

where k, m correspond to semantic descriptions of image K and image M. note that if the attribute cannot be computed, the function returns 1.

2.2.3 The distance between the fragments of images

As we already know, the image fragment is described by a vector $\vec{v} = \{x_1..x_k\}$, where each element is a code describing some properties of this fragment (tables 2-6). Being able to compare the elements of this vector (1), we can introduce a function of distance between the vectors k,m, that describes a rectangular fragment of the image (2).

$$\rho^{k,m} = \sum_{i=1}^{N} h_i^{km}, \quad (2)$$

Using (2) the distance between identical fragments, in terms of their semantic descriptions, will be equal to zero, and the maximum distance between the fragments is equal to N – the number of elements in the vector, which describes any fragment of an image.

2.2.4 A measure of the closeness between semantic descriptions of images

In order to establish the degree of "similarity" of images in terms of their semantic descriptions, it is necessary to establish a measure of the closeness between them, which, as in the case of the description of image fragments for identical descriptions would give 0, and for all the other a number > 0.

The Hausdorff Measure. Hausdorff distance (HD) [6] is a metric between two sets. As an example, consider two sets of points in the plane $A = \{a_1 \ldots a_m\}$ and $B = \{b_1 \ldots b_n\}$. In this case, the Hausdorff distance between these two sets of points is defined as:

$$H(A,B) = \max\big(h(A,B), h(B,A)\big), \quad (3)$$

$$h(A,B) = \max_{a \in A} \min_{b \in B} \|a - b\|. \quad (4)$$

Here h(A,B) is called a "directed Hausdorff distance" from A set A to the set B. A modified Hausdorff measure. For many applications, including for our search task measures the closeness between the semantic descriptions of the images, it is possible to apply the so-called "a modified Hausdorff measure" (5), it differs from (3) is that instead of the maximum distance it uses the average distance from set A to set B.

$$h_{mod}(A,B) = \frac{1}{|A|} \sum_{a \in A} \min_{b \in B} \|a - b\|, \quad (5)$$

Substituting in (5) expression (2) by using (1), we get the expression (6), which we will be used in the expression for the proximity measure between the semantic descriptions of the image (3), which can be used to assess the degree of similarity of two images.

$$h_{mod}(A,B) = \frac{1}{|A|} \sum_{a \in A} \min_{b \in B} \sum_{i=1}^{N} h_i^{ab}, \quad (6)$$

where h_i^{ab} is i-th code corresponding to the vectors a and b describing the fragments of two different images.

3 Summary

1. Using the concept of distance between images, we can find the "semantically similar" between images or videos.
2. Using the semantic analyzer of images presented in the paper gives the opportunity to create an indexed database of video information that include not only images, but also an additional set of metadata that can be obtained automatically during analysis of the image or video semantic analyzer, and which characterize an image or video.
3. Using the thus obtained additional information, you can organize a quick search for the desired video or image based on its semantic characteristics only.

References

1. R. Duda, P. Hart, «Pattern Classification and Scene Analysis», NY, 1973.
2. U.Prett «Digital Image Processing».
3. Paul A. Viola, Michael J. Jones Rapid Object Detection using a Boosted Cascade of Simple Features// CVPR (1) 2001: pp. 511-518
4. Bellustin N.S., Kalafati Y.D., Kovalchuck A.V., Telnykh A.A., Shemagina O.V., Yakhno V.G Neuropodobny detector litsa. Technicheskie osobennosti realisatsii I obuchenia// X Vserossiaiskaya nauchno-technicheskaya konferentsija "Neiroinformatika-2008", Sbornik trudov, Tschast 2 MIFI, Moskva, yanv. 2008, p 123-132
5. N.Bellustin, A. Kovalchuck, A. Telnykh, O. Shemagina, V.Yakhno, Y. Kalafati, Abhishek Vaish, Pinki Sharma, Shirshu Verma Instant Human Face Attributes Recognition System // (IJACSA) International Journal of Advanced Computer Science and Applications, Special Issue on Artificial Intelligence, pp.112-120

6. Oliver Jesorsky, Klaus J. Kirchberg, and Robert W. Frischholz Robust Face Detection using the Hausdorff Distance // Third International Conference on Audio- and Video-based Biometric Person Authentication, Springer, Lecture Notes in Computer Science, LNCS-2091, pp. 90–95, Halmstad, Sweden, 6–8 June 2001

AUTHOR INDEX

EDP Sciences – Web of Conferences
17, Avenue du Hoggar
Parc d'Activité de Courtabouf
BP 112
F-91944 Les Ulis Cedex A
France

CURRAN ASSOCIATES INC.
proceedings.com

ISBN 978-1-5108-3281-7
9 781510 832817